# THE BLENDED DRINK HANDBOOK

## 101 DELICIOUS BLENDS FOR HEALTHFUL LIVING

Pascoe Publishing, Inc.
Rocklin, California

Nutritional Analyses: Calculations for the nutritional analyses in this book are based on the largest number of servings listed within the recipes. Calculations are rounded up to the nearest gram or milligram, as appropriate. If two options for an ingredient are listed, the first one is used. Not included are optional ingredients or serving suggestions.

Design: KB Designs
Photography: Austin Blanco

Published in the United States of America by:

Pascoe Publishing, Inc.
Rocklin, California
www.pascoepublishing.com

ISBN: 978-1-929862-96-2

10      9      8      7      6      5      4      3      2      1

Printed in China

# TABLE OF CONTENTS

# INTRODUCTION

WHETHER YOU'RE ON THE GO, entertaining, or relaxing at home we've got the perfect drink for you! This isn't any ordinary book of recipes; it's your hand guide to the ultimate healthful drinks custom blended just for you.

Each recipe contains ingredients that combine to give you specific healthful benefits for the boost your body needs! Although our goal was to develop "healthy" recipes, our most important requirement was for each recipe to taste great!

*INSIDE THESE PAGES WE REVEAL* how to combine ingredients to obtain the maximum healthful benefits from delicious and flavorful recipes. Our **Health Highlights System** will help you to discover the incredible benefits of Super Foods that appeal to your body's nutrition as much as to your taste buds! How? The color-coded tabs for each recipe highlight which benefits you'll receive by making the recipe. From keeping your mind sharp to keeping your skin young, health highlights unlock your kitchen's potential to help you live a healthier lifestyle!

The next few pages are your guide to understanding the Health Highlights and also showcase the Food Glossary and Tips to rule the kitchen like a pro! So, go on…plug in your Ninja™ and blend delicious smoothies, juice whole fruits and vegetables, and create crowd pleasing cocktails! Above all… unlock the power of food and let our complete system inspire and simplify healthy living for your active on-the-go lifestyle.

You are what you drink, so here's to good health!

Cheers,

*The Ninja® Team*

HEALTH HIGHLIGHTS

ANTI-INFLAMMATORY

IMMUNE BOOST

MENTAL BOOST

RELAXATION & STRESS RELIEF

ANTI-AGING: SKIN, HAIR & EYE HEALTH

DETOXIFY & MANAGE WEIGHT

DIGESTION

ENERGY BOOST

Inflammation is usually associated with swelling, redness and pain, but it's also your body's first response to infection. It is linked to poor eating habits and obesity. If eaten on a regular basis, anti-inflammatory foods help bring a balance to inflammation in your body.

ANTI-INFLAMMATORY

"Antioxidants" seems to be a buzz word these days, but what's the real benefit? First, antioxidants fight off the over-production of free radicals. Second, these super-nutrients promote good health by fighting infections and diseases. And, in addition, they provide energy and even support skin health!

IMMUNE BOOST

Some days you feel like you're ready to take on the world… other days you feel like you're in a fog, un-motivated, and you find it hard to focus. When you're having one of "those" days, enjoy brain-boosting foods to help you feel more alert and focused.

MENTAL BOOST

A bit of relaxation can go a long way and these foods help your body to naturally relax. These foods might not help you meet a deadline or pay off your mortgage any faster, but they will help you feel more calm and cool. Eat your way to a less stressful life!.

RELAXATION & STRESS RELIEF

We all want truly fabulous skin, but who wants to pay hundreds of dollars for the latest skin cream, hair treatment, or spa day? Certain foods can help your skin look more radiant, your hair shinier, and do we dare say… help you look younger?!

ANTI-AGING: SKIN, HAIR & EYE HEALTH

These foods will help your body naturally filter, cleanse, and extract nutrients efficiently. Certain foods have natural cleansing properties that help rid your body of the extra junk you put in and can help naturally curb your appetite!

DETOXIFY & MANAGE WEIGHT

Many digestive-related problems are directly associated with what you eat. These foods can help naturally balance your digestive system, provide digestive-related aid, and are high in nutritional value.

DIGESTION

Have you ever been so tired at work that you fall asleep at your desk? Or even worse, nod off in a meeting? Keep these foods stashed at your desk to help fill you up, provide natural energy, and stay alert.

ENERGY BOOST

## ANTI-INFLAMMATORY SUPER FOODS

| VEGETABLES | | FRUITS | HERBS & NUTS | |
|---|---|---|---|---|
| Avocado | Green Onion | Apples | Almonds | Mint |
| Bell Pepper | Kale | Blueberries | Basil | Mustard |
| Bok Choy | Leeks | Guavas | Cayenne | Oregano |
| Broccoli | Olives | Kiwi | Cinnamon | Parsley |
| Brussels Sprouts | Spinach | Lemons | Cocoa | Rosemary |
| Cabbage | Sweet Potato | Limes | Flaxseed | Sunflower Seeds |
| Cauliflower | Swiss Chard | Oranges | Garlic | Thyme |
| Celery | Tomato | Papaya | Hazelnut | Walnuts |
| Fennel | Turnip Greens | Pineapple | Licorice | |
| Green Beans | | Raspberries | | |
| | | Strawberries | | |

## IMMUNE BOOSTER SUPER FOODS

| VEGETABLES | | FRUITS | | HERBS & NUTS | |
|---|---|---|---|---|---|
| Artichoke | Peppers | Acai Berry | Lemon | Almond | Sage |
| Beans | Pumpkin | Apple | Mango | Basil | Thyme |
| Broccoli | Squash | Apricot | Orange | Cayenne | Turmeric |
| Brussels Sprouts | Sweet Potato | Blackberry | Peach | Cinnamon | |
| Cabbage | Tomato | Blueberry | Pineapple | Flaxseed | |
| Carrot | | Cherry | Plum | Garlic | |
| Celery | | Coconut | Pomegranate | Ginger | |
| Cucumber | | Cranberry | Raspberry | Horseradish | |
| Green Beans | | Goji Berry | Strawberry | Oregano | |
| Kale | | Grape | Tangerine | Pecan | |
| Mushroom | | Grapefruit | Watermelon | | |
| | | Kiwi | | | |

## MENTAL BOOSTER SUPER FOODS

| VEGETABLES | FRUITS | | HERBS & NUTS |
| --- | --- | --- | --- |
| Arugula | Acai Berry | Lemon | Almond |
| Avocado | Apple | Lime | Cashew |
| Beets | Apricot | Mango | Coffee Bean |
| Broccoli | Banana | Orange | Flaxseed |
| Carrot | Blackberry | Plum | Horseradish |
| Eggplant | Blueberry | Raspberry | Peanut |
| Kale | Cantaloupe | Strawberry | Pumpkin Seed |
| Radish | Cherry | Watermelon | Rosemary |
| Romaine | Cranberry | | Sage |
| Spinach | Goji Berry | | Turmeric |
| Swiss Chard | Grapefruit | | Walnut |
| Tomato | | | |

## RELAXATION & STRESS REDUCER SUPER FOODS

| VEGETABLES | | FRUITS | HERBS & NUTS |
| --- | --- | --- | --- |
| Artichokes | Kale | Apple | Almond |
| Asparagus | Lentil | Apricot | Basil |
| Avocado | Spinach | Banana | Mint |
| Black Beans | Sweet Potato | Blueberry | Pistachio |
| Broccoli | Swiss Chard | Cherry | Pumpkin Seed |
| Brussels Sprouts | | Goji Berry | Sunflower Seed |
| Cabbage | | Orange | Walnut |
| Celery | | Papaya | |
| Chickpeas | | Pineapple | |
| Corn | | Pomegranate | |

## ANTI-AGING & SKIN, EYE, HAIR HEALTH SUPER FOODS

| VEGETABLES | | FRUITS | | HERBS & NUTS |
| --- | --- | --- | --- | --- |
| Artichoke | Peppers | Acai Berry | Mango | Almond |
| Asparagus | Radish | Blackberry | Orange | Cinnamon |
| Avocado | Red Onion | Blueberry | Papaya | Flaxseed |
| Beet | Spinach | Cantaloupe | Peach | Garlic |
| Bok Choy | Squash | Cherry | Pineapple | Ginger |
| Broccoli | Sweet Potato | Cranberry | Plum | Macadamia Nut |
| Brussels Sprouts | Tomato | Goji Berry | Pomegranate | Parsley |
| Cabbage | Turnip | Grape | Raspberry | Pumpkin Seed |
| Carrot | | Grapefruit | Strawberry | Sage |
| Cauliflower | | Guava | Watermelon | Sesame Seed |
| Celery | | Honeydew | | Sunflower Seed |
| Cucumber | | Kiwi | | Turmeric |
| Kale | | | | Walnut |

## DETOXIFY & WEIGHT MANAGEMENT SUPER FOODS

| VEGETABLES | | FRUITS | | HERBS & NUTS |
| --- | --- | --- | --- | --- |
| Artichoke | Lettuce | Apple | Lemon | Cayenne |
| Asparagus | Mushroom | Blackberry | Papaya | Chili Pepper |
| Beans | Okra | Blueberry | Pineapple | Cinnamon |
| Beet | Peppers | Cantaloupe | Pomegranate | Dill |
| Broccoli | Spinach | Cherry | Prunes | Flaxseed |
| Cabbage | Sweet Potato | Coconut | Raspberry | Ginger |
| Carrot | Tomato | Goji Berry | Strawberry | Horseradish |
| Cauliflower | Yam | Grape | Watermelon | Mint |
| Celery | | Grapefruit | | Mustard |
| Cucumber | | Guava | | Pine Nut |
| Fennel | | Kiwi | | Sage |
| Green Bean | | | | Sesame Seed |

## DIGESTION SUPER FOODS

| VEGETABLES | FRUITS | | HERBS & NUTS | |
|---|---|---|---|---|
| Artichoke | Apple | Lemon | Basil | Ginger |
| Avocado | Banana | Papaya | Chickpea | Mint |
| Beet | Blackberry | Pear | Cinnamon | Oregano |
| Broccoli | Blueberry | Pineapple | Coriander | Paprika |
| Cabbage | Cherry | Prune | Cumin | Sage |
| Cucumber | Cranberry | | Curry | Sunflower Seed |
| Lettuce | Goji Berry | | Dill | |
| Okra | Grape | | Fennel | |
| Onion | Grapefruit | | Flaxseed | |
| Squash | Guava | | Garlic | |
| Sweet Potato | | | | |

## ENERGY BOOST SUPER FOODS

| VEGETABLES | FRUITS | | HERBS & NUTS |
|---|---|---|---|
| Avocado | Apple | Pear | Almond |
| Beans | Banana | Raspberry | Cashew |
| Celery | Blackberry | Strawberry | Cilantro |
| Corn | Blueberry | Watermelon | Flaxseed |
| Cucumber | Cantaloupe | | Hazelnut |
| Kale | Coconut | | Parsley |
| Lettuce | Grapefruit | | Pumpkin Seed |
| Mushroom | Kiwi | | |
| Spinach | Lemon | | |
| Squash | Orange | | |
| Sweet Potato | | | |

## APPLES

THE ADVANTAGE:
- Really strong antioxidant power!
- A true healing-power food
- The second-highest level of antioxidant activity of any consumed fruit
- Valuable source of fiber, which can lower cholesterol
- Contains the highest source of Boron, a mineral that assists in bone-building.

FOOD FOR THOUGHT:
- The apple peel has the most potent antioxidant activity.
- Purchased apple juice may have added sugar and preservatives, along with higher calories. Make your own at home as the best alternative.

## BANANAS

THE ADVANTAGE:
- Bananas are a rich source of Vitamin B6, which may prolong mental health, according to the USDA.
- High in potassium and fiber

FOOD FOR THOUGHT:
- Bananas are rich in potassium, which can help maintain body fluids, assist heart health, balance electrolytes, reduce muscle cramps, and elevate energy levels.
- Assists in good digestive health.
- The inner peel is one of the most nutritional parts! Scrape the inner peel into your smoothie for an added nutritional boost!

RELAXATION & STRESS RELIEF

DIGESTION

ENERGY BOOST

## BLUEBERRIES

THE ADVANTAGE:
- This little fruit packs a big punch that helps keep your memory sharp and your brain stimulated.
- One of the most powerful fruits to include in your diet
- Blueberries provide strong antioxidant power, act as an anti-inflammatory, and may help with your memory.

FOOD FOR THOUGHT:
- Either fresh or frozen berries deliver the same delicious, healthy benefits.
- Blue and Purple fruit are memory-boosters.

| CANTALOUPE | RASPBERRIES | STRAWBERRIES |
|---|---|---|

**CANTALOUPE**

THE ADVANTAGE:
- Cantaloupe is your best friend in weight control. Why? It is a high-volume fruit that curbs hunger: high in fiber, water and air, yet low in calories. Your body thinks you're full faster, with less craving for more.
- Rich in potassium and Vitamin A, which helps heart-health, blood pressure, vision, growth and bone-building.
- High in Vitamin C!
- One of the best immune boosters among all fruits!

FOOD FOR THOUGHT:
- Cantaloupe is rich in Vitamin A as a beta carotene. It helps protect against cell damage and is a great antioxidant.

TASTE THE ADVANTAGE:
- Mix cantaloupe with watermelon, club soda, and fresh ginger for a refreshing treat.

**RASPBERRIES**

THE ADVANTAGE:
- A fiber powerhouse!
- The benefits don't stop there; raspberries have magnesium and, not to mention, are low in calories.
- Help replace dying cells with healthy cells, may help with inflammation and pain.
- Significant antioxidant boost.

FOOD FOR THOUGHT:
- This fruit is fragile: we recommend buying fresh and organic for best nutritional value and flavor satisfaction.
- Highest count of fiber among the most commonly eaten berries.

**STRAWBERRIES**

THE ADVANTAGE:
- Potent antioxidant berry.
- Offers the most Vitamin C of any other commonly consumed berry.
- Red fruits can help improve blood flow and are thought to help prevent Alzheimer's disease.

FOOD FOR THOUGHT:
- 1 cup of strawberries equals about 50 calories and offers around 3g of fiber and around 85mg of Vitamin C.
- Noted as one of the most contaminated fruits. Buy organic to get the best flavor and quality.
- Frozen strawberries offer the same health benefits as fresh, a great alternative year round.
- High in disease-fighting phytochemicals.

| PINEAPPLE | ORANGES | KIWI |
|---|---|---|

**THE ADVANTAGE:**

- Powerful anti-inflammatory powers.
- Contains Bromelain enzymes, natural blood thinners, that can aid in digestion, healing and inflammation.
- Provides fiber, Vitamin C, potassium, and other minerals for general good health.
- Yellow and Orange fruits help prevent eye disease and act as an immune boost.

**FOOD FOR THOUGHT:**

- One of the most powerful natural digestive reliefs.
- 1 cup of fresh pineapple has almost 100% of the daily value for manganese. Manganese is essential for healthy skin, cartilage formation and bones.

**THE ADVANTAGE:**

- A massive boost of Vitamin C, a premier antioxidant.
- Provides support for better heart and digestive health and lowers the risk of infections, inflammation and stroke.
- May also improve healthful cholesterol.
- Contains high amounts of calcium, which promotes strong bones and teeth.

**FOOD FOR THOUGHT:**

- Studies have shown citrus fruits may lower the risk of some cancers.
- Pulp is your friend! Pulp contains the healthiest nutrients in fruits, providing many vitamin compounds, minerals and fiber.

**THE ADVANTAGE:**

- A super-fruit, rich with antioxidants, that can help in healing.
- Kiwis have the highest level of Vitamin C, twice that of oranges.
- A good source of Vitamin E, potassium, and fiber.

**FOOD FOR THOUGHT:**

- Kiwi works as a natural blood thinner.
- Green fruits can help protect bones and teeth, and aid in eyesight.
- A natural meat tenderizer, cut kiwi in half and rub on meat before cooking.

## WATERMELON

**THE ADVANTAGE:**
- One of the healthiest foods! Watermelon helps curb your appetite and provides high levels of lycopene and Vitamin A.
- A high-volume food which aids in managing weight.
- Great source of vitamin A as a beta-carotene that helps fight free radicals, essential for eye and immune health.

**FOOD FOR THOUGHT:**
- Helps support eye and immune health via Vitamin A (in beta-carotene), which helps fight free radicals.
- Watermelon is great after a workout. It can help re-hydrate your body and restore electrolyte balance.

IMMUNE BOOST

MENTAL BOOST

ANTI-AGING

DETOXIFY & MANAGE WEIGHT

## AVOCADOS

**THE ADVANTAGE:**
- Although high in fat; the fact is, it's a healthy HDL fat. Monounsaturated fat is an omega-9 that may actually lower cholesterol.
- Contains lutein from the carotene family that acts as an antioxidant to aid in eye, heart and skin health.
- Avocados are a great source of fiber, potassium, folate, Vitamin A, Vitamin E, Zinc and beta-carotene.
- Rich in folate, in the Vitamin B family, that may help prevent birth defects.

**FOOD FOR THOUGHT:**
- Research studies link avocados to lower blood pressure and cholesterol counts. Helpful in maintaining bone and immune health.

ANTI-INFLAMMATORY

RELAXATION & STRESS RELIEF

ANTI-AGING

DIGESTION

## KALE

**THE ADVANTAGE:**
- Superstar vegetable! The #1 antioxidant food that fights cell-damaging free radicals.
- Contains phyto-chemicals that have been shown to have protective effects against many cancers.
- Loaded with calcium, Vitamin A, C, K, and iron.
- Terrific source of fiber and protein.

**FOOD FOR THOUGHT:**
- Kale has seven times the beta-carotene of broccoli.

ANTI-INFLAMMATORY

IMMUNE BOOST

MENTAL BOOST

RELAXATION & STRESS RELIEF

ANTI-AGING

## TOMATOES

THE ADVANTAGE:

- Provides extremely beneficial anti-cancer properties when consumed with fat-rich foods such as avocados. Fat-rich foods help the absorption of lycopene.
- Tomatoes contain multiple antioxidant agents that have strong disease fighting power.
- A mega dose of Vitamin C, rich in potassium and magnesium, this powerful combo is a great choice to restore your body after a workout.

FOOD FOR THOUGHT:

- May be especially good for men; the antioxidant compounds have been shown to fight prostate cancer.

IMMUNE BOOST
MENTAL BOOST
ANTI-AGING
DETOXIFY & MANAGE WEIGHT

## SPINACH

THE ADVANTAGE:

- One of the best sources of Vitamin K, critical for building strong bones. Vitamin K works with calcium to make sure you get the minerals into your bones.
- It's also rich in Vitamin A, manganese, folic acid, magnesium, iron, and quercetin (anti-inflamatory compound).
- Promotes good health as an antioxidant and anti-cancer support.
- May help lower cholesterol and blood pressure while assisting eye and heart-health. Can also help reduce inflammation.

FOOD FOR THOUGHT:

- Spinach provides more nutrients than almost any other food.
- One of the lowest calorie foods on the planet.
- A great alternative to milk for Vitamin C.

ANTI-INFLAMMATORY
IMMUNE BOOST
MENTAL BOOST
RELAXATION & STRESS RELIEF
ANTI-AGING
DETOXIFY & MANAGE WEIGHT
ENERGY BOOST

## BROCCOLI

THE ADVANTAGE:

- Strong antioxidant and aid in detoxifying.
- 1 cup of broccoli contains more than 40mg of calcium, 81 mg of Vitamin C, 2g of protein and fiber, a whopping 1,277 mcg of Vitamin A, plus folate, magnesium, phosphorus and beta-carotene.
- Great for bone, teeth, and eye health.

FOOD FOR THOUGHT:

- Broccoli has been shown to help fight cancers by neutralizing carcinogens that destroy cancerous cells.
- May be especially good for women; broccoli is linked to reducing the risk of breast and cervical cancer.

ANTI-INFLAMMATORY
IMMUNE BOOST
MENTAL BOOST
RELAXATION & STRESS RELIEF
ANTI-AGING
DETOXIFY & MANAGE WEIGHT

## CARROTS

THE ADVANTAGE:
- Contains a high level of carotenoids, which are associated with decreasing the risk of cancer.
- A great source of lutein, which provides eye health.
- Antioxidant and immune system stimulator, helpful in fighting infections.
- Rich source of calcium, potassium, Vitamin A and sprinkled with magnesium, phosphorus and fiber.
- Fantastic for detoxifying!

FOOD FOR THOUGHT:
- Recent studies have indicated a carrot a day could cut the rate of lung cancer.
- Yellow and Orange fruits help with eye health and can boost your immune system.

**IMMUNE BOOST**

**MENTAL BOOST**

**ANTI-AGING**

**DETOXIFY & MANAGE WEIGHT**

# FRUIT & VEGETABLE CHART

This handy chart lists quick tips to select, store and prep fruit and vegetables before using.
Save precious nutrients (and money) by following these simple tips to get the best results:

| FRUIT/VEGETABLE: | CHOOSE: | STORE: | PREP: |
|---|---|---|---|
| APPLE | ripe, crisp fruit | • Refrigerate – up to 6 weeks<br>• Room temp – up to 1 week | Wash just before using; Remove core, stem; Keep peel to retain nutrients; Cut into fourths or more to blend; Use lemon juice to avoid browning |
| APRICOT | soft tender skin | • Refrigerate – up to 2 days<br>• Room temp – up to 2 days | Wash just before using; Peel, remove pit; Cut in half to blend |
| BANANA | yellow, firm fruit | • Refrigerate – not recommended<br>• Room temp – up to 1 week<br>• Ripens at room temp<br>• Freeze overripe bananas for later use | Peel; Cut in half to blend |
| BERRIES | firm fruit | • In a single layer<br>• Refrigerate – up to 2 days<br>• Room temp – up to 2 days | Wash just before using; If needed, remove hull, leaves |
| GRAPEFRUIT | heavy, firm, thin-skinned fruit | • Refrigerator – up to 3 weeks<br>• Room temp – up to 1 week | Wash just before using; Peel and section; Remove any seeds |
| GRAPES | firm, plump fruit | • Refrigerate – up to 2 weeks<br>• Room temp – up to 2 days | Wash just before using; Remove stems |
| KIWI | slightly firm fruit, with fuzzy skin | • Refrigerate – up to 6 weeks in plastic bag | Wash before using; Peel; Cut in half to blend |
| LEMON/LIME | thin skin, firm and heavy | • Refrigerate – up to 2 weeks<br>• Room temp – up to 1 week | Wash before using; Peel; Remove seeds |
| MANGO | slightly firm fruit with sweet aroma | • Refrigerate - peeled fruit up to 2 days<br>• Room temp - unpeeled fruit up to 2 days | Wash before using; Peel; Remove pit |
| MELON | firm flesh, slight pebbled texture, sweet aroma | • Refrigerate - up to 5 days<br>• Room temp - whole, uncut fruit up to 2 weeks | Wash before using; Peel; Remove seeds and any pith; Cut in large chunks to blend |

| | | | |
|---|---|---|---|
| ORANGE/ TANGERINE | "heavy for size" fruit | • Refrigerate - up to 3 weeks<br>• Room temp - up to 1 week | Wash before using; Peel; Remove any seeds and pith; Section fruit to blend |
| PAPAYA | firm fruit, slight yellow streaks | • Refrigerate - peeled up to 2 days<br>• Room temp - unpeeled 2 to 3 days until totally yellow/orange | Wash before using; Peel; Remove seeds and pith; Cut in large chunks to blend |
| PEACH | firm, fuzzy skin; slightly soft to touch | • Refrigerate – up to 2 days<br>• Room temp – store in paper bag until ripe | Wash before using; Peel; Remove pit; Slice or cut in chunks to blend |
| PEAR | slightly firm fruit with sweet aroma | • Refrigerate – peeled up to 2 days<br>• Room temp – unpeeled up to 1 week; fruit ripens on standing | Wash before using; No need to peel; Remove core and seeds; Slice or cut into chunks to blend |
| PINEAPPLE | firm fruit with dark leaves; small inner leaf pulls out easily when ripe | • Refrigerate – peeled up to 2 days<br>• Room temp – unpeeled up to 1 day | Wash before using; Peel; Remove core; Cut into chunks to blend |
| PLUM | smooth, soft skins | • Refrigerate – up to 1 week<br>• Room temp – store unripe plums in paper bag to ripen up to 3 days | Wash before using; No need to peel; Remove pit; Slice or cut into chunks to blend |
| RASPBERRIES | firm, plump berries | • Refrigerate – up to 2 days<br>• Room temp – not recommended | Wash just before using; Remove leaves or stems |
| STRAWBERRIES | firm, shiny red fuit with healthy green caps | • Refrigerate – up to 3 days<br>• Room temp – not recommended | Wash just before using; Remove caps and hull, if desired |
| WATERMELON | heavy fruit with dried stems, light underside | • Refrigerate – peeled melon for up to 5 days in plastic bag<br>• Room temp – unpeeled up to 2 days | Wash before using; Peel rind; Remove seeds, if desired; Cut in large chunks to blend |
| ARTICHOKES | firm, tightly closed leaves | • Refrigerate – in plastic bag up to 1 week<br>• Room temp – up to 3 days | Wash before using; Steam until tender; Cut heart in large chunks to blend |
| ARUGULA | bright green leaves | • Refrigerate – loosely wrapped in damp paper towels up to 3 days<br>• Room temp – not recommended | Rinse before using; Remove moldy or discolored leaves; Tear into large pieces to blend |
| ASPARAGUS | thin, dry, firm stalks | • Refrigerate – wrap in damp paper towel in plastic bag for up to 4 days<br>• Room temp – not recommended | Wash just before using; Snap off tough ends; Use raw or steam until tender; Slice or snap into 2-inch pieces to blend |

| | | | |
|---|---|---|---|
| AVOCADO | slightly firm, rich, pebbled skin | • Refrigerate – cut up to 2 days<br>• Room temp – ripen unpeeled in a paper bag up to 3 days | Wash before using; Peel; Remove pit; Cut in half to blend |
| BEETS | small, firm with fresh leaves | • Refrigerate – leaves in plastic bag up to 1 week; root up to 1 week<br>• Room temp – not recommended | Wash leaves, root before using; Cut leaves 1-inch from root, use fresh or steam; Cut root ends; steam until tender; Cut in chunks to blend |
| BOK CHOY | firm, fresh stalks | • Refrigerate – up to 1 week in damp paper towel<br>• Room temp – not recommended | Wash just before using; Remove wilted leaves; Use fresh or steam until tender; Cut in large pieces to blend |
| BROCCOLI | firm, tight buds, healthy leaves | Refrigerate – unwashed up to 10 days<br>Room temp – not recommended | Wash just before using; Cut away tough ends; snap into small buds; Use fresh or steam until tender; Cut into 1-inch pieces to blend |
| BUTTERNUT SQUASH | heavy, firm with smooth skin | • Refrigerate – peeled or cut up to 3 days<br>• Room temp – unpeeled up to 1 month in dark, cool place | Wash before using; Remove outer peel; Remove seeds, pith; Steam until tender; Cut into large chunks to blend |
| CABBAGE | firm, heavy for size, compact leaves | • Refrigerate – up to 1 week<br>• Room temp – not recommended | Wash before using; Remove wilted leaves; Remove core; Use fresh or steam until tender; Cut in large chunks to blend |
| CARROTS | firm, crisp, deep-orange colored | • Refrigerate – in plastic bag up to 2 weeks (remove tops)<br>• Room temp – not recommended | Wash before using; Cut off root end and tip; Use fresh or steam until tender; Cut into 1-inch pieces to blend |
| CAULIFLOWER | compact buds, bright leaves | • Refrigerate – in plastic bag up to 1 week<br>• Room temp – not recommended | Wash before using; Remove tough end, leaves; Use fresh or steam until tender; Cut into large chunks to blend |
| CELERY | bright green, crisp stalks | • Refrigerate – in plastic bag up to 1 week<br>• Room temp – not recommended | Wash before using; Use fresh or steam until tender; Cut into 2-inch pieces to blend |
| CORN | tight corn on cobs, fresh silk | • Refrigerate – in husks up to 2 days<br>• Room temp – not recommended | Remove husks, silk; Steam until tender; Cut from cob before blending |
| CUCUMBER | uniform dark green, firm skin | • Refrigerate – in plastic bag up to 1 week<br>• Room temp – not recommended | Wash before using; Peel; Cut into large chunks to blend |

| | | | |
|---|---|---|---|
| FENNEL | bright bulbs, dark green leaves | • Refrigerate – in plastic bag up to 5 days<br>• Room temp – not recommended | Wash before using; Discard stalks, unless using; Peel away yellow layers; Cut into 1-inch pieces to blend |
| GARLIC | firm, plump bulbs, white in color | • Refrigerator – not recommended<br>• Room temp – in skin up to 8 weeks in cool, dry place | Peel skin; Cut off root end; Toss in whole to blend |
| GREEN BEANS | uniformly green, snap easily when bent | • Refrigerate – in plastic bag up to 1 week<br>• Room temp – not recommended | Wash before using; Snap or cut off ends; Use fresh or steam until tender; Cut in half to blend |
| GREENS (ALL VARIETIES) | bright green leaves | • Refrigerate – in plastic bag up to 1 week<br>• Room temp – not recommended | Wash thoroughly before using; Tear into pieces; Use fresh or steam until tender; Tear into large pieces to blend |
| MUSHROOMS | firm, smooth, tight gills | • Refrigerate – unwashed in paper bag up to 3 days<br>• Room temp – not recommended | Brush off visible dirt; Cut off bottom; Slice or cut as needed; Use fresh or steam until tender; Toss in whole to blend |
| ONIONS | tight skins, symmetrical shape | • Refrigerate – cut up to 2 weeks<br>• Room temp – unpeeled in a cool, dark place up to 1 month | Peel outer layers; Wash before using; Cut root top and bottom; Use fresh or steam until tender; Cut in large chunks to blend |
| PEAS | bright green pods | • Refrigerate – in perforated bag up to 5 days<br>• Room temp – not recommended | Shell just before using; Wash before using; Use fresh or steam until tender; Toss in whole to blend |
| PEPPERS | firm, bright colors | • Refrigerate – in plastic bag up to 5 days<br>• Room temp – not recommended | Wash before using; Cut away top, core, seeds, white pith; Use fresh or steam until tender; Cut into large chunks to Pulse |
| SPINACH | uniform green leaves | • Refrigerate – in plastic bag up to 1 week<br>• Room temp – not recommended | Wash before using; Cut off stems, if desired; Toss in whole to blend |
| SQUASH (AND PUMPKIN) | bright colors, firm, heavy for size | • Refrigerate – cut in plastic bag up to 3 days<br>• Room temp – uncut in cool, dry place up to 3 months | Wash before using; Peel rind; Remove seeds, pith; Use fresh, or steam until tender; Cut into large chunks to blend |
| SWISS CHARD | uniform, dark green leaves | • Refrigerate – in plastic bag up to 3 days<br>• Room temp – not recommended | Wash thoroughly before using; Cut or tear pieces; Remove inner spine, if desired; Use fresh or steam until tender; Tear into pieces to blend |

# MAKE YOUR OWN *natural* NON-DAIRY MILK!

makes 4 cups
## FRESH RICE MILK

Use organic white or brown rice as the base for this light non-dairy milk.

1 CUP COOKED WHITE OR BROWN RICE, COOLED
4 CUPS WATER
1 TBSP. MAPLE SYRUP OR HONEY
½ TSP. PURE VANILLA EXTRACT

Place the rice and 1 cup water in the pitcher; blend until smooth. Add the remaining water, honey and vanilla and blend again for 10 seconds.

Strain over cheesecloth and reserve the milk. Refrigerate the milk for up to 3 days.

per serving: cal 51; fat 0g; chol 0mg; sodium 0mg; carb 11g; fiber 0g; protein 0g

makes 4 to 5 cups
## FRESH COCONUT MILK

A rich and delicious creamy milk can be made from coconuts. Use a hammer and nail to open the nuts and capture the coconut water.

MEAT FROM 2 COCONUTS, INNER BROWN PEEL
    REMOVED
4½ CUPS WARM WATER, DIVIDED

Place the coconut and 1 cup water in the pitcher. Blend until smooth; add 1 cup water. Blend again. Add the remaining water and blend again.

Strain over cheesecloth and discard solids, or if thinner milk is desired, add more water to the solids and blend and strain again. Refrigerate the milk for up to 4 days.

per serving: cal 248; fat 26g; chol 0mg; sodium 16mg; carb 6g; fiber 2g; protein 2g

 Coconut milk, with a rich and naturally sweet flavor, has more fat and calories than coconut water.

# FRESH ALMOND MILK

Easy to make, with no preservatives!

1½ CUPS RAW, BLANCHED ALMONDS
4 TO 5 CUPS WATER, DIVIDED
2 TBSP. HONEY, DIVIDED
1 TSP. VANILLA EXTRACT (OPTIONAL)
PINCH GROUND CINNAMON (OPTIONAL)

Place the almonds in the pitcher and cover with water. Blend until smooth; add honey, vanilla and cinnamon. Blend again.

Strain the milk over cheesecloth into a bowl and set aside. Spoon the almond meal back into the pitcher and add up to 1½ cups water. Blend again and add the remaining honey. Strain and add the liquid to the reserved milk. Refrigerate for up to 3 days.

per serving: cal 45; fat 2g; chol 0mg; sodium 113mg; carb 6g; fiber 1g; protein 1g

# YOUR BALANCING ACT

*(reducing infection; increasing defenses)*

2

IMMUNE BOOST

MENTAL BOOST

ANTI-AGING: SKIN, HAIR & EYE HEALTH

DETOXIFY & MANAGE WEIGHT

DIGESTION

serves 1 to 2

# CHERRY CRANBERRY CREATION

Choose yogurt containing live cultures, which break down the lactose in the milk, offering better digestion and assimilation into your system.

⅔ CUP ICE CUBES
15 FRESH CHERRIES, STEMS REMOVED, PITTED
½ CUP CRANBERRY JUICE
½ CUP PLAIN GREEK YOGURT

**Place all of the of the ingredients in the Single Serve Cup and blend until smooth.**

per serving: cal 387; fat 17g; chol 65mg; sodium 78mg; carb 44g; fiber 3g; protein 15g

serves 1 to 2

# VITAMIN B6 POPPER

Your immune system and metabolism will dance with the infusion of vitamin B6 found here! Make variations of this smoothie by using only spinach or kale instead of both, or mix it up by using other flavors of yogurt and juice.

½ CUP ICE CUBES
½ CUP APPLE JUICE
¼ CUP BABY SPINACH, PACKED
¼ CUP KALE, ROUGHLY TORN, PACKED
6 OZ. VANILLA YOGURT (LOWFAT OR REGULAR)

**Place all of the of the ingredients in the Single Serve Cup and blend until smooth.**

per serving: cal 221; fat 3g; chol 10mg; sodium 100mg; carb 56g; fiber 3g; protein 12g;

ANTI-INFLAMMATORY

IMMUNE BOOST

MENTAL BOOST

RELAXATION & STRESS RELIEF

ANTI-AGING: SKIN, HAIR & EYE HEALTH

DETOXIFY & MANAGE WEIGHT

ENERGY BOOST

ANTI-INFLAMMATORY

IMMUNE BOOST

MENTAL BOOST

RELAXATION & STRESS RELIEF

ANTI-AGING: SKIN, HAIR & EYE HEALTH

DETOXIFY & MANAGE WEIGHT

DIGESTION

ENERGY BOOST

serves 1 to 2

# SWEET-TART FUSION

The idea of drinking cabbage juice may not sound appealing, but trust us! This combination is sweet-tart and offers tons of immune-building properties. Strain this juice, if desired, but if you want to capture more of the nutrients, drink it without straining.

2 TO 3 ICE CUBES
½ SMALL APPLE, CORED, CUT IN CHUNKS
¼ SMALL CARROT, PEELED, CUT IN CHUNKS
½ CUP FRESH GREEN CABBAGE, ROUGHLY TORN
½ CUP WHITE GRAPE JUICE

Place the ice, apple and carrot in the Single Serve Cup and blend until smooth. Add the cabbage and grape juice and blend again.

per serving: cal 131; fat 0g; chol 0mg; sodium 19mg; carb 33g; fiber 3g; protein 1g

 Look for grape juice with no sugar added!

serves 1 to 2

# PEACHY PEAR POWER JUICE

Especially great for kids who will think this "power juice" is dandy, but might otherwise recoil if asked to eat green vegetables. Strain this juice when first serving to a child, then gradually work toward serving it un-strained for maximum nutritional benefit.

2 TO 3 ICE CUBES
½ SMALL, RIPE PEAR, CORED, QUARTERED
½ SMALL, RIPE PEACH, PITTED, CUT IN HALF
¼ CUP COLLARD GREENS, PACKED
½ CUP PEAR OR PEACH JUICE (OR ANY FRUIT JUICE
     YOU HAVE HANDY)

**Place all of the of the ingredients in the Single Serve Cup and blend until smooth.**

per serving: cal 142; fat 0g; chol 0mg; sodium 6mg; carb 46g; fiber 6g; protein 0g

ANTI-INFLAMMATORY

IMMUNE BOOST

MENTAL BOOST

ANTI-AGING: SKIN, HAIR & EYE HEALTH

DIGESTION

ENERGY BOOST

ANTI-INFLAMMATORY

IMMUNE BOOST

RELAXATION & STRESS RELIEF

ANTI-AGING: SKIN, HAIR & EYE HEALTH

DETOXIFY & MANAGE WEIGHT

DIGESTION

serves 3 to 4

# PINEAPPLE EXPRESS

Bromelain, an enzyme found in pineapple, actually helps repair muscles when injured and helps heal bruises rapidly. This is your go-to smoothie when you need fast repair work!

1 CUP ICE CUBES

1 CUP FRESH PINEAPPLE, CUT IN CHUNKS
    (OR USE FROZEN OR CANNED PINEAPPLE)

1 CUP PINEAPPLE JUICE

1 CUP PLAIN GREEK YOGURT

4 TBSP. CRUNCHY GRANOLA, OPTIONAL

Place all of the ingredients, except the granola, in the pitcher. Blend until smooth. Spoon or pour into glasses and garnish each with the granola, if desired

per serving: cal 234; fat 9g; chol 33mg; sodium 34mg; carb 32g; fiber 1g; protein 8g

serves 2

# IMMUNI-TEA

Feeling kind of weak after a flu bug or infection?
This is your recovery juice to build up immunity
against all the other bugs out there calling your
name.

2 CUPS GREEN TEA, COOLED AND FROZEN
    UNTIL FIRM
1 CUCUMBER, PEELED, CUT IN CHUNKS
6 MINT LEAVES
DASH GROUND GINGER
DASH GROUND CLOVES

**Place all of the ingredients in the pitcher.
Blend until smooth.**

per serving: cal 17; fat 0g; chol 0mg; sodium 3mg;
carb 3g; fiber 1g; protein 1g

ANTI-INFLAMMATORY

IMMUNE BOOST

ANTI-AGING: SKIN, HAIR & EYE HEALTH

DETOXIFY & MANAGE WEIGHT

DIGESTION

ENERGY BOOST

ANTI-INFLAMMATORY

IMMUNE BOOST

MENTAL BOOST

RELAXATION & STRESS RELIEF

ANTI-AGING: SKIN, HAIR & EYE HEALTH

DETOXIFY & MANAGE WEIGHT

DIGESTION

ENERGY BOOST

serves 1

# POMEGRANATE POWER SMOOTHIE

A little touch of honey adds just the right amount of sweetness!

½ CUP LOWFAT PLAIN YOGURT
½ CUP POMEGRANATE JUICE
½ CUP FROZEN BLUEBERRIES
1 TBSP. RAW, UNFILTERED HONEY

**Place all of the of the ingredients in the Single Serve Cup and blend until smooth.**

per serving: cal 223; fat 2g; chol 7mg; sodium 118mg;
carb 50g; fiber 2g; protein 7g

serves 2

# KALE & DATE SMOOTHIE

The ingredients in this smoothie make it a great immune booster!

1½ CUPS FRESH ORANGE JUICE
1 CUP NONFAT VANILLA YOGURT
1 BANANA, PEELED
1 CUP FRESH KALE, TIGHTLY PACKED
2 DATES, PITTED
10 TO 12 ICE CUBES

**Place all ingredients in the pitcher and blend until smooth. Serve right away.**

per serving: cal 363; fat 0g; chol 3mg; sodium 101mg; carb 87g; fiber 6g; protein 9g

ANTI-INFLAMMATORY

IMMUNE BOOST

MENTAL BOOST

RELAXATION & STRESS RELIEF

ANTI-AGING: SKIN, HAIR & EYE HEALTH

DETOXIFY & MANAGE WEIGHT

DIGESTION

ENERGY BOOST

IMMUNE BOOST

MENTAL BOOST

ANTI-AGING: SKIN, HAIR & EYE HEALTH

DIGESTION

ENERGY BOOST

serves 4

# MANGO LASSI

A tropical treat to enjoy any time of day.

2 CUPS MANGO CHUNKS, FROZEN
2 CUPS LOWFAT PLAIN YOGURT
1 CUP MANGO JUICE OR MILK
4 TSP. RAW, UNFILTERED HONEY
⅛ TSP. PINCH CARDAMOM

**Place all ingredients in the pitcher and blend until smooth.**

per serving: cal 225; fat 2g; chol 7mg; sodium 92mg; carb 47g; fiber 2g; protein 6g

serves 3 to 4

# HEART-HAPPY JUICE COCKTAIL

Chock-full of good vitamins and minerals, this juice will help strengthen those important muscles, even that tender heart!

4 TO 6 ICE CUBES
1 RIPE TOMATO, CORED, CUT IN HALF
½ CUP FRESH SPINACH, LIGHTLY PACKED
½ CUP KALE, LIGHTLY PACKED
6 SLICES FRESH APPLE, PEELED (ABOUT 1 CUP)
⅛ TSP SALT
⅛ TSP BLACK PEPPER
1 CUP FILTERED WATER

Place all of the ingredients in the pitcher. Blend until smooth. Strain, if desired, before serving.

per serving: cal 52; fat 0g; chol 0mg; sodium 42mg;
carb 11g; fiber 3g; protein 3g

ANTI-INFLAMMATORY

IMMUNE BOOST

MENTAL BOOST

RELAXATION & STRESS RELIEF

ANTI-AGING: SKIN, HAIR & EYE HEALTH

DETOXIFY & MANAGE WEIGHT

DIGESTION

ENERGY BOOST

serves 2 to 3

# CITRUS SPIRULINA BLAST

A fresh blast of citrus pumped up with a hit of spirulina.

1 GRAPEFRUIT, PEELED AND QUARTERED
1 ORANGE, PEELED AND QUARTERED
1 CUP FRESH OR FROZEN PINEAPPLE,
    CUT IN CHUNKS
2 TBSP. LIME JUICE
1 TSP. SPIRULINA
1 CUP WATER
6 TO 8 ICE CUBES

**Place all ingredients in the pitcher and blend until smooth. Serve right away.**

per serving: cal 84; fat 0g; chol 0mg; sodium 1mg; carb 21g; fiber 3g; protein 1g

serves 1 to 2

# A GREEN & GOLD AFFAIR

Like a favorite plaid shirt, this juice of many colors is also mighty good for you. Vitamin A, B, C, and D are all are included and ready to get the party started! Strain this juice if you must, but you'll get more benefits by drinking it without straining first. We're just saying…

2 TO 3 ICE CUBES
½ RIPE GALA APPLE, CORED, CUT IN CHUNKS
½ SMALL ORANGE, PEELED, SEGMENTED
¼ CUP COLLARD GREENS, ROUGHLY TORN, PACKED (OR USE ANY MIXED GREENS)
¼ CUP WATER

Place all of the of the ingredients in the Single Serve Cup and blend until smooth.

per serving: cal 70; fat 0g; chol 0mg; sodium 1mg;
carb 18g; fiber 4g; protein 1g

ANTI-INFLAMMATORY

IMMUNE BOOST

MENTAL BOOST

RELAXATION & STRESS RELIEF

ANTI-AGING: SKIN, HAIR & EYE HEALTH

DIGESTION

ENERGY BOOST

ANTI-INFLAMMATORY

IMMUNE BOOST

MENTAL BOOST

RELAXATION & STRESS RELIEF

ANTI-AGING: SKIN, HAIR & EYE HEALTH

DETOXIFY & MANAGE WEIGHT

ENERGY BOOST

serves 1 to 2

# SHOT OF SUPER C

Packing almost 200 milligrams of vitamin C, this shot is the perfect way to build immunity!

½ CUP ICE CUBES
½ SMALL NAVAL ORANGE, PEELED (OR USE TANGELOS OR MINNEOLAS)
½ SMALL GRAPEFRUIT, PEELED
½ CUP PINEAPPLE JUICE

**Place all of the of the ingredients in the Single Serve Cup and blend until smooth.**

per serving: cal 152; fat 0g; chol 0mg; sodium 4mg;
carb 37g; fiber 2g; protein 3g

# WORKING OUT!
*(rehydrating; power up)*

3

ANTI-INFLAMMATORY

IMMUNE BOOST

MENTAL BOOST

RELAXATION & STRESS RELIEF

ANTI-AGING: SKIN, HAIR & EYE HEALTH

ENERGY BOOST

serves 1 to 2

# CRANBERRY & ORANGE COOLER

Cranberry juice and naturally sweet oranges tag-team in this smoothie to bring a super dose of vitamin C, infection prevention and reviving power to your day! Buy natural, unsweetened cranberry juice, if possible.

½ CUP ICE CUBES
½ MEDIUM ORANGE, PEELED, SEGMENTED
6 OZ. RASPBERRY YOGURT
½ CUP CRANBERRY JUICE

**Place all of the of the ingredients in the Single Serve Cup and blend until smooth.**

per serving: cal 251; fat 2g; chol 5mg; sodium 133mg;
carb 54g; fiber 3g; protein 7g

serves 1 to 2

# FREQUENT FLYER SMOOTHIE

Does your life go up and down like a roller coaster? Try this delicious, turbulence-free smoothie.

½ CUP ICE CUBES
1 KIWI, PEELED, CUT IN HALF
½ MEDIUM ORANGE, PEELED, CUT IN HALF
¾ CUP ORANGE JUICE
½ SMALL BANANA, PEELED

**Place all of the of the ingredients in the Single Serve Cup and blend until smooth.**

per serving: cal 169; fat 0g; chol 0mg; sodium 2mg; carb 29g; fiber 6g; protein 4g

 Make your own orange juice by blending a peeled, sectioned orange with 3 to 4 ice cubes.

ANTI-INFLAMMATORY

IMMUNE BOOST

MENTAL BOOST

RELAXATION & STRESS RELIEF

ANTI-AGING: SKIN, HAIR & EYE HEALTH

DIGESTION

ENERGY BOOST

ANTI-INFLAMMATORY

IMMUNE BOOST

MENTAL BOOST

RELAXATION & STRESS RELIEF

ANTI-AGING: SKIN, HAIR & EYE HEALTH

ENERGY BOOST

serves 2

# CREAMY EGG WHIP

If you want to seriously power-up and build strength, this egg whip may be your best breakfast ever. Whenever you choose to consume raw eggs, use only pasteurized eggs to avoid the risk of illness from bacteria. You'll find pasteurized eggs in grocery stores everywhere.

½ CUP ICE CUBES
2 PASTEURIZED EGGS
6 OZ. LOWFAT VANILLA YOGURT
¼ CUP ORANGE JUICE
1 TSP. HONEY

**Place all of the of the ingredients in the Single Serve Cup and blend until smooth.**

per serving: cal 359; fat 11g; chol 337mg; sodium 232mg; carb 46g; fiber 0g; protein 19g

serves 1 to 2

# STRAWBERRY BENCH PRESS

Funny thing about bananas; they give your heart a serious boost of potassium. And, just as nice, strawberries are big antioxidant fighters. The icing on the cake? A spoonful of wheat germ offers fiber and helps you feel full until your next meal.

½ CUP ICE CUBES

½ SMALL BANANA, PEELED

½ CUP STRAWBERRIES, HULLED

1 TBSP. WHEAT GERM

½ CUP ORANGE BANANA JUICE
   (OR USE ANY FRUIT JUICE)

**Place all of the of the ingredients in the Single Serve Cup and blend until smooth.**

per serving: cal 244; fat 3g; chol 0mg; sodium 8mg; carb 49g; fiber 7g; protein 10g

ANTI-INFLAMMATORY

IMMUNE BOOST

MENTAL BOOST

RELAXATION & STRESS RELIEF

ANTI-AGING: SKIN, HAIR & EYE HEALTH

DETOXIFY & MANAGE WEIGHT

DIGESTION

ENERGY BOOST

IMMUNE BOOST

MENTAL BOOST

ANTI-AGING: SKIN, HAIR & EYE HEALTH

DETOXIFY & MANAGE WEIGHT

DIGESTION

ENERGY BOOST

serves 1 to 2

# C & C WORK OUT

Time to work out? Gear up with fresh celery and carrots…just skip the ranch-flavored dipping sauce.

½ MEDIUM CARROT, SCRUBBED, CUT IN FOURTHS
1 RIB CELERY, CUT IN FOURTHS
½ CUP CUCUMBER, PEELED, CUT IN FOURTHS
¼ CUP GREEN GRAPES
½ CUP SWEETENED GREEN TEA, COOLED

Place all of the of the ingredients in the Single Serve Cup and blend until smooth. Strain, if desired, before serving.

per serving: cal 56; fat 0g; chol 0mg; sodium 47mg;
carb 12g; fiber 3g; protein 1g

ANTI-INFLAMMATORY

IMMUNE BOOST

MENTAL BOOST

ANTI-AGING: SKIN, HAIR & EYE HEALTH

DETOXIFY & MANAGE WEIGHT

serves 1 to 2

# TOMATO HYDRATION STATION

Replenish your system with high-water content vegetables and tart fruit juice. You'll get more nutrients by drinking this juice without straining, but your kids will probably like it better if you do.

2 TO 3 ICE CUBES
1 MEDIUM RIPE TOMATO, CORED, QUARTERED
½ SMALL CARROT, SCRUBBED, CUT IN THIRDS
1 TSP. LEMON JUICE
½ CUP ORANGE JUICE

**Place all of the of the ingredients in the Single Serve Cup and blend until smooth.**

per serving: cal 104; fat 0g; chol 0mg; sodium 42mg; carb 24g; fiber 3g; protein 3g

 Fully grown carrots and their cousins, parsnips, can be topped and kept in cold storage for up to 5 months.

ANTI-INFLAMMATORY

IMMUNE BOOST

MENTAL BOOST

RELAXATION & STRESS RELIEF

ANTI-AGING: SKIN, HAIR & EYE HEALTH

DETOXIFY & MANAGE WEIGHT

DIGESTION

ENERGY BOOST

serves 2 to 3

# MELON & MINT TWISTER

Rehydrating after exercising is a priority – blend these simple ingredients until smooth and enjoy the surge of energy!

4 ICE CUBES
1 CUP WATERMELON, CUT IN CHUNKS
1 CUP HONEYDEW MELON, CUT IN CHUNKS
6 MINT LEAVES
1 MEDIUM ORANGE, PEELED, SEGMENTED

Place all of the ingredients in the pitcher. Blend until smooth.  Strain, if desired, before serving.

per serving: cal 125; fat 0g; chol 0mg; sodium 24mg; carb 31g; fiber 4g; protein 3g

serves 3 to 4

# 5 MINUTE REVIVAL

Silky rich and fragrantly sweet, this little drink will revive your senses in the most subtle, unassuming way.

1 RIPE PAPAYA, PEELED, SEEDED, QUARTERED
2 SMALL BANANAS, PEELED, CUT IN HALF
3 TO 4 TSP. LEMON JUICE
2 CUPS CHILLED LOWFAT BUTTERMILK
    (OR USE MILK)

**Place the papaya, banana, lemon juice and buttermilk in the pitcher. Blend until smooth.**

per serving: cal 230; fat 2g; chol 10mg; sodium 13mg; carb 46g; fiber 4g; protein 9g

 Substitute lowfat or fat-free buttermilk!

ANTI-INFLAMMATORY

MENTAL BOOST

RELAXATION & STRESS RELIEF

DETOXIFY & MANAGE WEIGHT

DIGESTION

ENERGY BOOST

ANTI-INFLAMMATORY

IMMUNE BOOST

MENTAL BOOST

RELAXATION & STRESS RELIEF

ANTI-AGING: SKIN, HAIR & EYE HEALTH

DETOXIFY & MANAGE WEIGHT

DIGESTION

ENERGY BOOST

serves 4

# DANDY GREEN MACHINE

Blend these healthy ingredients together, taste to confirm the great flavor and then sit back and enjoy.

2 CUPS APPLE JUICE
2 CUPS SWISS CHARD, RINSED, ROUGHLY TORN
2 BANANAS, PEELED
8 TBSP. GOJI BERRIES
24 TO 32 ICE CUBES

**Place the ingredients in the pitcher and blend until smooth.  Serve right away.**

per serving: cal 220; fat 1g; chol 0mg; sodium 115mg; carb 54g; fiber 6g; protein 5g

serves 4

# PEANUT BUTTER CHOCOLATE SMOOTHIE

Yummy chocolate & peanut butter blended together for a delicious treat.

1 CUP LOWFAT MILK
8 TBSP. CREAMY PEANUT BUTTER
3 CUPS LOWFAT VANILLA FROZEN YOGURT
4 OZ. DARK CHOCOLATE

**Place all ingredients in the pitcher and blend until smooth. Serve right away.**

per serving: cal 395; fat 18g; chol 5mg; sodium 239mg; carb 61g; fiber 10g; protein 15g

ANTI-INFLAMMATORY

IMMUNE BOOST

ANTI-AGING: SKIN, HAIR & EYE HEALTH

DIGESTION

ENERGY BOOST

ANTI-INFLAMMATORY

IMMUNE BOOST

MENTAL BOOST

RELAXATION & STRESS RELIEF

DETOXIFY & MANAGE WEIGHT

DIGESTION

ENERGY BOOST

serves 4

# CARROT PROTEIN POWDER

Whey protein....is the ideal ingredient before or after a work out.

2 CUPS APPLE JUICE
2 SMALL CARROTS, ROUGHLY CUT
1 SMALL RIPE GRANNY SMITH APPLE
2 BANANAS, PEELED
4 TBSP. WHEY PROTEIN POWDER
20 TO 24 ICE CUBES

Place all ingredients in the pitcher and blend until smooth. Strain before serving if desired.

per serving: cal 271; fat 2g; chol 60mg; sodium 93mg; carb 46g; fiber 5g; protein 19g

serves 3 to 4

# COMPLETE SUPER IRON JUICE

A refreshing juice for any time of day.

8 TO 12 ICE CUBES
1 CUCUMBER, PEELED
1 STALK CELERY, CUT IN HALF
2 TART GREEN APPLES, CORED
1 CUP PACKED SPINACH LEAVES
2 CUPS WATER

Place the ingredients in the pitcher and blend until smooth.

per serving: cal 55; fat 0g; chol 0mg; sodium 11mg; carb 13g; fiber 2g; protein 0g

ANTI-INFLAMMATORY

IMMUNE BOOST

MENTAL BOOST

RELAXATION & STRESS RELIEF

ANTI-AGING: SKIN, HAIR & EYE HEALTH

DETOXIFY & MANAGE WEIGHT

DIGESTION

ENERGY BOOST

IMMUNE BOOST

MENTAL BOOST

ANTI-AGING: SKIN, HAIR & EYE HEALTH

DETOXIFY & MANAGE WEIGHT

DIGESTION

ENERGY BOOST

serves 4

# COMPLETE AFTERBURNER JUICE

Perfect refreshment after a workout!

4 CUPS GREEN GRAPES
8 MEDIUM LEAVES ROMAINE LETTUCE
1 CUCUMBER, PEELED
2 CUPS WATER
12 TO 16 ICE CUBES

Place all ingredients in the pitcher and blend until smooth.

per serving: cal 110; fat 0g; chol 0mg; sodium 5mg; carb 28g; fiber 1g; protein 1g

serves 4

# APPLE GINGER GLADIATOR

Cool and clean flavors with a wheat grass bonus.

2 APPLES CORED, CUT IN QUARTERS
2 TSP. FRESH GINGER
2 OZ. WHEAT GRASS JUICE
1 CUP WATER
4 TO 6 ICE CUBES

Place the apple, ginger and wheat grass in the pitcher and blend until smooth. Add the water and ice cubes and blend again until smooth. Serve right away.

per serving: cal 84; fat 0g; chol 0mg; sodium 1mg; carb 21g; fiber 2g; protein 1g

ANTI-INFLAMMATORY

IMMUNE BOOST

MENTAL BOOST

RELAXATION & STRESS RELIEF

ANTI-AGING, SKIN, HAIR & EYE HEALTH

DETOXIFY & MANAGE WEIGHT

DIGESTION

ENERGY BOOST

ANTI-INFLAMMATORY

IMMUNE BOOST

MENTAL BOOST

RELAXATION & STRESS RELIEF

ANTI-AGING: SKIN, HAIR & EYE HEALTH

DETOXIFY & MANAGE WEIGHT

DIGESTION

ENERGY BOOST

serves 3 to 4

# MINTY CUCUMBER COOLER

This light drink is as refreshing as it sounds. Great as an after-workout boost!

2 CUCUMBERS, PEELED AND ROUGHLY CHOPPED
4 TBSP. LEMON JUICE
4 TBSP. FRESH MINT LEAVES
4 TBSP. AGAVE
4 TO 6 ICE CUBES

Place all ingredients in the pitcher and blend until smooth. Serve right away.

per serving: cal 70; fat 0g; chol 0mg; sodium 2mg; carb 18g; fiber 1g; protein 1g

# BRAIN-POWER BLENDING

*(mind over matter)*

MENTAL BOOST

RELAXATION & STRESS RELIEF

DIGESTION

ENERGY BOOST

serves 1 to 2

# BANANA & PEAR LIFT

A simple, yet very satisfying smoothie for any time of the day! Mix it up by substituting strawberries or other fruit for the pear, or toss in a few walnuts to add to the super-nutrient value.

½ CUP ICE CUBES

½ SMALL RIPE BARTLETT OR ANJOU PEAR, CORED, CUT IN HALF

½ BANANA, PEELED

6 OZ. VANILLA YOGURT

½ CUP PEAR OR APPLE JUICE

2 TBSP. CRUNCHY GRANOLA, OPTIONAL

Place all ingredients, except the granola, in the Single Serve Cup. Blend until very smooth. Sprinkle the granola over the smoothie before serving, if desired.

per serving: cal 320; fat 3g; chol 10mg; sodium 107mg; carb 70g; fiber 4g; protein 8g

serves 1 to 2

# BLUEBERRY BANANA COLD FUSION

Toss out those granny glasses! Studies have proven that blueberries are a helpful factor in preventing macular degeneration, glaucoma and cataracts. They also help keep your memory sharp and are sweetly delicious.

½ CUP ICE CUBES
½ CUP FROZEN BLUEBERRIES
½ SMALL BANANA, PEELED
½ CUP ORANGE-BANANA JUICE
   (OR USE ORANGE JUICE)

**Place all of the of the ingredients in the Single Serve Cup and blend until smooth.**

per serving: cal 147; fat 0g; chol 0mg; sodium 7mg; carb 38g; fiber 4g; protein 3g

ANTI-INFLAMMATORY

IMMUNE BOOST

MENTAL BOOST

RELAXATION & STRESS RELIEF

ANTI-AGING: SKIN, HAIR & EYE HEALTH

DETOXIFY & MANAGE WEIGHT

DIGESTION

ENERGY BOOST

ANTI-INFLAMMATORY

IMMUNE BOOST

MENTAL BOOST

RELAXATION & STRESS RELIEF

ANTI-AGING: SKIN, HAIR & EYE HEALTH

DETOXIFY & MANAGE WEIGHT

DIGESTION

ENERGY BOOST

serves 1 to 2

# STRAWBERRY FIELDS

When you can't get enough of a good thing, this thick, rich strawberry delight is your go-to smoothie.  Add 1 or 2 tablespoons of milk to the recipe if you like a more pourable consistency.

½ CUP ICE CUBES
½ CUP FRESH STRAWBERRIES, HULLED
½ MEDIUM BANANA, PEELED
6 OZ. STRAWBERRY YOGURT
2 TBSP. LOWFAT MILK OR SOYMILK

**Place all of the of the ingredients in the Single Serve Cup and blend until smooth.**

per serving: cal 264; fat 4g; chol 2mg; sodium 22mg;
carb 134g; fiber 31g; protein 9g

serves 1 to 2

# MANGO MENTAL BOOST

Sure, mangos are delicious, but did you know they also contain lots of potassium and great vitamins? Mangos have a high water content so they also help you feel full longer.

½ CUP FROZEN PEACHES, CUT IN CHUNKS
½ CUP FROZEN MANGOS, CUT IN CHUNKS
¾ CUP GREEN TEA, CHILLED
1 TSP. HONEY

**Place all of the of the ingredients in the Single Serve Cup and blend until smooth.**

per serving: cal 91; fat 0g; chol 0mg; sodium 2mg;
carb 2g; fiber 3g; protein 0g

 Green tea is loaded with polyphenols, antioxidants that help rid the body of free radicals. In other words, it's good for you!

ANTI-INFLAMMATORY

IMMUNE BOOST

MENTAL BOOST

RELAXATION & STRESS RELIEF

ANTI-AGING: SKIN, HAIR & EYE HEALTH

DETOXIFY & MANAGE WEIGHT

ENERGY BOOST

serves 1 to 2

# SPINACH JOLT JUICE

Get a powerful brain boost in this easy juice!

2 TO 3 ICE CUBES
½ CUP FRESH SPINACH LEAVES, LIGHTLY PACKED
½ RIB CELERY, CUT IN HALF
½ CUP GREEN GRAPES
½ CUP WHITE GRAPE JUICE

Place the ice, spinach, celery, grapes and juice in the Single Serve Cup.  Blend until smooth.

per serving: cal 115; fat 0g; chol 0mg; sodium 26mg; carb 29g; fiber 0g; protein 0g

 Did you know darker green vegetables have more vitamin C than lighter green vegetables?

serves 1 to 2

# BERRY GOOD BLAST

Berries have high antioxidant and anti-inflammatory compounds, so this smoothie is the perfect way to start your day. Soft tofu adds an excellent boost of iron and protein.

½ CUP PLAIN OR VANILLA SOFT TOFU (OR USE
    SILKEN TOFU)
½ CUP FRESH BLUEBERRIES
½ CUP FRESH RASPBERRIES
½ CUP APPLE JUICE

**Place all ingredients in the Single Serve Cup. Blend until smooth.**

per serving: cal 195; fat 3g; chol 0mg; sodium 7mg; carb 37g; fiber 6g; protein 2g

ANTI-INFLAMMATORY

IMMUNE BOOST

MENTAL BOOST

RELAXATION & STRESS RELIEF

ANTI-AGING: SKIN, HAIR & EYE HEALTH

DETOXIFY & MANAGE WEIGHT

DIGESTION

ENERGY BOOST

ANTI-INFLAMMATORY

IMMUNE BOOST

MENTAL BOOST

RELAXATION & STRESS RELIEF

ANTI-AGING: SKIN, HAIR & EYE HEALTH

DETOXIFY & MANAGE WEIGHT

DIGESTION

ENERGY BOOST

serves 1 to 2

# ABC JUICE

Apples, broccoli and carrots – oh my!  All of these provide a great way to sharpen your child's focus at school and power up the day.  Kids typically like juice when strained, but unstrained juice has more nutrients, so work toward that goal, if possible.

2 TO 3 ICE CUBES
¾ CUP APPLE JUICE
½ MEDIUM FUJI APPLE, CORED, CUT IN CHUNKS
¼ CUP BROCCOLI FLORETS
¼ SMALL CARROT, SCRUBBED WELL,
    CUT IN CHUNKS

**Place all of the ingredients in the Single Serve Cup.  Blend until smooth. Strain, if desired, before serving.**

per serving: cal 174; fat 0g; chol 0mg; sodium 54mg; carb 43g; fiber 6g; protein 2g

serves 4

# LEMON PICK-UP

This tart smoothie packs a great dose of vitamin C, along with anti-inflammatory properties and the added jolt of energy from black tea.

1 CUP ICE CUBES
12 OZ. VANILLA YOGURT
1½ CUPS STRONG BLACK TEA, CHILLED
4 TBSP. LEMON JUICE
2 TO 4 TSP. HONEY (OR TO TASTE)

**Place the ice cubes, yogurt, tea and lemon juice in the pitcher and add the honey to taste.  Blend until smooth.**

per serving: cal 174; fat 3g; chol 10mg; sodium 100mg; carb 36g; fiber 0g; protein 7g

 Try using chai tea for a flavorful twist.

ANTI-INFLAMMATORY

IMMUNE BOOST

MENTAL BOOST

DIGESTION

ENERGY BOOST

ANTI-INFLAMMATORY

IMMUNE BOOST

MENTAL BOOST

RELAXATION & STRESS RELIEF

DIGESTION

ENERGY BOOST

serves 3 to 4

# PUMPKIN GINGER SMOOTHIE

Pumpkin is incredibly rich in antioxidants and vitamins and low in calories.  Perfect in the fall when there are pumpkins galore.

1 CUP PUMPKIN PUREE

1 CUP ORANGE JUICE

1 CUP LOWFAT VANILLA YOGURT

¼ TSP. FRESH GINGER

⅛ TSP. GROUND CINNAMON (OPTIONAL)

2 TSP. RAW, UNFILTERED HONEY (OPTIONAL)

10 TO 12 ICE CUBES

**Place all ingredients in the pitcher and blend until smooth.**

per serving: cal 364, fat 0g, chol 4mg, sodium 403mg, carb 84g, fiber 11g, protein 3g

ANTI-INFLAMMATORY

IMMUNE BOOST

MENTAL BOOST

RELAXATION & STRESS RELIEF

ANTI-AGING: SKIN, HAIR & EYE HEALTH

ENERGY BOOST

serves 3 to 4

# QUICK ORANGESICLE

The summer memory of a popsicle, fudgesicle or orangesicle. This recipe is creamy and dreamy.

2 CUPS LOWFAT VANILLA FROZEN YOGURT
½ CUP ORANGE JUICE
1 CUP FRESH ORANGE, PEELED, SEGMENTED

**Place all ingredients in the pitcher and blend until smooth. Serve right away.**

per serving: cal 287, fat 0g, chol 4mg, sodium 122mg, carb 64g, fiber 3g, protein 1g

ANTI-INFLAMMATORY

IMMUNE BOOST

MENTAL BOOST

RELAXATION & STRESS RELIEF

DETOXIFY & MANAGE WEIGHT

DIGESTION

ENERGY BOOST

serves 4

# GARDEN VEGGIES IN A GLASS

Blend up these veggies and you will have a powerhouse of flavor. Want to spice it up even more – just add a dash of your favorite hot sauce.

2 CUPS APPLE JUICE
2 SMALL RIPE TOMATOES, PEELED,
    CUT IN HALF
2 INNER STALK CELERY, WITH LEAVES
4 TBSP. FRESH FLAT-LEAF PARSLEY
2 GREEN ONIONS, ROUGHLY CUT
¼ PINCH SALT
1 TSP. GROUND BLACK PEPPER

Place all ingredients in the pitcher and blend until smooth. Strain before serving, if desired.

per serving: cal 78, fat 0g, chol 0mg, sodium 165mg, carb 16g, fiber 2g, protein 1g

serves 4

# MANGO MELON MINT FUSION

All these M's add up to Mmmmmmm!

1 CUP HONEYDEW MELON, CUT IN CHUNKS
1 CUP MANGO, CUT IN CHUNKS
1 CUP CANTALOUPE, CUT IN CHUNKS
6 MINT LEAVES
1 CUP WATER
6 TO 8 ICE CUBES

**Place all ingredients in the pitcher and blend until smooth. Serve immediately.**

per serving: cal 47; fat 0g; chol 0mg; sodium 18mg;
carb 10g; fiber 2g; protein 2g

ANTI-INFLAMMATORY

MENTAL BOOST

RELAXATION & STRESS RELIEF

ANTI-AGING-SKIN, HAIR & EYE HEALTH

DETOXIFY & MANAGE WEIGHT

DIGESTION

ENERGY BOOST

ANTI-INFLAMMATORY

IMMUNE BOOST

MENTAL BOOST

RELAXATION & STRESS RELIEF

ANTI-AGING: SKIN, HAIR & EYE HEALTH

DETOXIFY & MANAGE WEIGHT

DIGESTION

ENERGY BOOST

serves 3 to 4

# MORNING OAT SMOOTHIE

A great on-the-go breakfast!

1 CUP STEEL CUT OATS, SOAKED OVERNIGHT
1 FROZEN BANANA, PEELED
4 TBSP. TOASTED ALMONDS
4 TBSP. ORGANIC RAISINS
2 TBSP. AGAVE
1 CUP FAT-FREE FROZEN VANILLA YOGURT
½ CUP WATER

**Place all ingredients in the pitcher and blend until smooth. Serve right away.**

per serving: cal 73; fat 0g; chol 1mg; sodium 32mg; carb 16g; fiber 1g; protein 2g

 Change up the flavor by using almond or banana yogurt.

# STRESS-BUSTERS

*(the no-anxiety/no -stress zone)*

5

MENTAL BOOST

RELAXATION & STRESS RELIEF

DIGESTION

ENERGY BOOST

serves 1 to 2

# BACKYARD HAMMOCK SMOOTHIE

Bananas are high in carbohydrates and rich in potassium, both of which make your heart very happy.  And, the carbs in this soothing smoothie help you feel full longer, which means your nap in the hammock can last a long, long time.

½ CUP ICE CUBES
1 SMALL BANANA, PEELED, CUT IN HALF
6 OZ. LEMON YOGURT (OR USE ANY FRUIT
　　FLAVORED YOGURT)
¾ CUP LOWFAT MILK

Place all ingredients in the Single Serve Cup. Blend until icy and smooth.

per serving: cal 417; fat 7g; chol 30mg; sodium 216mg; carb 76g; fiber 3g; protein 17g

ANTI-INFLAMMATORY

IMMUNE BOOST

MENTAL BOOST

RELAXATION & STRESS RELIEF

ANTI-AGING-SKIN, HAIR & EYE HEALTH

DIGESTION

serves 1 to 2

# VACATION IN MY MIND

Toss in a tablespoon of oatmeal or wheat germ to thicken the smoothie and keep you going strong all day.

½ CUP ICE CUBES
2 RIPE APRICOTS, PEELED, PITTED, CUT IN HALF
   (OR USE 1 NECTARINE OR PEACH)
½ CUP APPLE JUICE
6 OZ. PEACH YOGURT

**Place all of the of the ingredients in the Single Serve Cup and blend until smooth.**

per serving: cal 263; fat 3g; chol 15mg; sodium 107mg; carb 52g; fiber 1g; protein 9g

 Just 1 ounce of apricot fruit has enough beta-carotene to supply 20% of your daily vitamin A requirements.

ANTI-INFLAMMATORY

IMMUNE BOOST

MENTAL BOOST

RELAXATION & STRESS RELIEF

ANTI-AGING: SKIN, HAIR & EYE HEALTH

DETOXIFY & MANAGE WEIGHT

DIGESTION

serves 1 to 2

# BANANA & PAPAYA STRESS BUSTER

The perfect start to a busy workday! Buy frozen mangos and papayas, or peel and seed fresh fruit and freeze in chunks so you'll always have a supply on hand.

½ SMALL BANANA, PEELED
½ CUP FROZEN PAPAYA, CUT IN CHUNKS
¼ CUP FROZEN MANGO, CUT IN CHUNKS
6 OZ. LEMON YOGURT
¾ CUP LEMONADE (OR USE LEMON-LIME
    GATORADE)

**Place all of the of the ingredients in the Single Serve Cup and blend until smooth.**

per serving: cal 272; fat 2g; chol 11mg; sodium 109mg; carb 46g; fiber 3g; protein 9g

ANTI-INFLAMMATORY

MENTAL BOOST

RELAXATION & STRESS RELIEF

DETOXIFY & MANAGE WEIGHT

DIGESTION

serves 1 to 2

# COCONUT LIME JUICE

Use unsweetened coconut milk for this juice – the papaya and lime add key tropical flavors.

3 TO 4 ICE CUBES
½ CUP UNSWEETENED COCONUT MILK
1 TSP. LIME JUICE
½ PAPAYA, SEEDED, PEELED, CUT IN CHUNKS

**Place the ice, coconut milk, juice and papaya in the Single Serve Cup. Blend until smooth.**

per serving: cal 77; fat 5g; chol 0mg; sodium 19mg; carb 9g; fiber 1g; protein 1g

 Unsweetened coconut milk has only 50 calories and 5 grams of fat per cup. Look for it in either shelf stable cartons or in the refrigerated case at your grocery store.

ANTI-INFLAMMATORY

IMMUNE BOOST

MENTAL BOOST

RELAXATION & STRESS RELIEF

ANTI-AGING: SKIN, HAIR & EYE HEALTH

DETOXIFY & MANAGE WEIGHT

ENERGY BOOST

serves 1 to 2

# KIWI GREEN GODDESS

Kiwi, apples and oranges are the major flavors in this juice. We kind of snuck in the spinach so no need to mention it to your kids. They'll love it!

2 ICE CUBES
1 LARGE KIWI, PEELED, CUT IN HALF
½ CUP FRESH SPINACH, TIGHTLY PACKED
½ CUP ORANGE JUICE
½ SMALL FUJI APPLE, CORED, QUARTERED

Place all of the ingredients in the Single Serve Cup. Blend until smooth. Strain the juice before serving, if desired.

per serving: cal 159; fat 0g; chol 0mg; sodium 17mg; carb 37g; fiber 5g; protein 2g

74

ANTI-INFLAMMATORY

IMMUNE BOOST

MENTAL BOOST

RELAXATION & STRESS RELIEF

ANTI-AGING: SKIN, HAIR & EYE HEALTH

DIGESTION

ENERGY BOOST

serves 1 to 2

# RELAXING SPLASH

A delightfully refreshing drink of pure fruit goodness!

2 TO 3 ICE CUBES

1 CUP CARBONATED WATER (OR USE SPARKLING
   UNSWEETENED FLAVORED WATER)

4 TBSP. FROZEN ORANGE JUICE CONCENTRATE, UNDILUTED

1 SMALL PEAR, CORED, QUARTERED

2 TO 4 MINT LEAVES

**Place all of the of the ingredients in the Single Serve Cup and blend until smooth.**

per serving: cal 307; fat 0g; chol 0mg; sodium 5mg;
carb 76g; fiber 5g; protein 4g

serves 3 to 4

# SWEET DREAMS JUICE

Although apples and oranges contain fructose, these natural sugars help assimilate the fresh spinach leaves into your system and aid in sleeping.

4 ICE CUBES
1 SMALL JOHNATHON OR GALA APPLE, QUARTERED
1 MEDIUM ORANGE, PEELED, SEGMENTED
½ CUP FRESH SPINACH LEAVES, LIGHTLY PACKED
1 CUP WATER (OR USE UNSWEETENED FLAVORED WATER)

Place all of the ingredients in the pitcher and blend until smooth.

per serving: cal 131; fat 0g; chol 0mg; sodium 3mg; carb 34g; fiber 1g; protein 1g

serves 4

# MANGO PINEAPPLE BLITZ

Fresh pineapple brings so much to your good health! It not only aids in keeping your digestive tract happy, it is chock full of great enzymes that help speed healing and reduce inflammation. Frozen and canned pineapple (in juice; not syrup) are also great sources, but fresh pineapple remains the best.

1 CUP FROZEN MANGO CHUNKS
6 LARGE SLICES FRESH PINEAPPLE (ABOUT 1½
    CUPS), PLUS MORE FOR GARNISH
1 CUP PINEAPPLE JUICE
4 TBSP. LIGHT CREAM (OR USE MILK)

Place all of the ingredients in the pitcher. Blend until very smooth. Pour into glasses and garnish with extra fresh pineapple.

per serving: cal 223; fat 4g; chol 11mg; sodium 19mg; carb 48g; fiber 3g; protein 3g

ANTI-INFLAMMATORY

IMMUNE BOOST

MENTAL BOOST

RELAXATION & STRESS RELIEF

ANTI-AGING-SKIN, HAIR & EYE HEALTH

DETOXIFY & MANAGE WEIGHT

DIGESTION

ANTI-INFLAMMATORY

IMMUNE BOOST

MENTAL BOOST

RELAXATION & STRESS RELIEF

ANTI-AGING: SKIN, HAIR & EYE HEALTH

DETOXIFY & MANAGE WEIGHT

DIGESTION

ENERGY BOOST

serves 4

# SUPER BLUEBERRY FREEZE

This quick and easy smoothie will totally satisfy those raging after-school appetites!

2 CUPS BLUEBERRIES
2 CUPS APPLE JUICE
3 CUPS FROZEN VANILLA YOGURT

**Place all ingredients in the pitcher and blend until smooth.**

per serving: cal 248; fat 0g; chol 0mg; sodium 122mg; carb 50g; fiber 9g; protein 8g

serves 2 to 3

# SWEET CHERRY SMOOTHIE

We put the cherries right into the smoothie but don't forget to hang a couple over the top of your glass for a perfect presentation!

1 CUP LOWFAT MILK

1 CUP LOWFAT VANILLA YOGURT

1 CUP FRESH SWEET CHERRIES, PITTED
     (OR USE FROZEN CHERRIES, IF DESIRED)

1 BANANA, PEELED

10 TO 12 ICE CUBES

**Place all ingredients in the pitcher and blend until smooth.**

per serving: cal 239; fat 2g; chol 10mg; sodium 134mg; carb 46g; fiber 12g; protein 10g

IMMUNE BOOST

MENTAL BOOST

RELAXATION & STRESS RELIEF

ANTI-AGING: SKIN, HAIR & EYE HEALTH

DETOXIFY & MANAGE WEIGHT

DIGESTION

ENERGY BOOST

ANTI-INFLAMMATORY

IMMUNE BOOST

MENTAL BOOST

RELAXATION & STRESS RELIEF

ANTI-AGING: SKIN, HAIR & EYE HEALTH

DETOXIFY & MANAGE WEIGHT

DIGESTION

ENERGY BOOST

serves 3 to 4

# CARROT APPLE REFRESHER

Refreshing! Refreshing! Refreshing! The blend of apples and carrots are sweetened up by just a bit of honey!

1 CUP CARROT JUICE
1 SMALL CARROT, PEELED, ROUGHLY CUT
1 SMALL RIPE GRANNY SMITH APPLE,
    PEELED, ROUGHLY CUT
½ CUP LOWFAT PLAIN YOGURT
2 TSP. RAW, UNFILTERED HONEY (OR TO TASTE)
PINCH GROUND CLOVES
10 TO 12 ICE CUBES

## Place all ingredients in the pitcher and blend until smooth.

per serving: cal 183; fat 0g; chol 2mg; sodium 93mg;
carb 26g; fiber 1g; protein 3g

# DRINK IT IN!
*(natural skin, hair and eye beauty-builders)*

6

ANTI-INFLAMMATORY

IMMUNE BOOST

MENTAL BOOST

RELAXATION & STRESS RELIEF

ANTI-AGING: SKIN, HAIR & EYE HEALTH

DETOXIFY & MANAGE WEIGHT

DIGESTION

ENERGY BOOST

serves 1 to 2

# BLACKBERRY LIGHT

Loaded with vitamins, minerals and fiber, blackberries are an easy way to help maintain your weight. Paired in this smoothie with yogurt and papaya, they are even better! Freeze blackberries when in season and pop a handful into any smoothie for great flavor.

½ CUP ICE CUBES
½ CUP BLACKBERRIES
½ CUP NONFAT LEMON YOGURT
½ RIPE PAPAYA, SEEDED, CUT IN CHUNKS
¼ CUP LOWFAT MILK

**Place all of the of the ingredients in the Single Serve Cup and blend until smooth.**

per serving: cal 257; fat 1g; chol 5mg; sodium 136mg; carb 51g; fiber 7g; protein 11g

serves 1 to 2

# LEAN N' MEAN SMOOTHIE

Berries and watermelon are tasty, refreshing and inviting, and at the same time, carry few calories and little fat. Adding a bit of nonfat Greek yogurt gives the fruit a nice tangy balance. Light indulgence!

½ CUP WATERMELON, CUT IN CHUNKS
½ CUP RASPBERRIES
½ CUP STRAWBERRIES, HULLED
6 OZ. NONFAT GREEK YOGURT (VANILLA OR
　　BERRY FLAVORED)

**Place all of the of the ingredients in the Single Serve Cup and blend until smooth.**

per serving: cal 212; fat 0g; chol 0mg; sodium 9mg; carb 35g; fiber 6g; protein 18g

ANTI-INFLAMMATORY

IMMUNE BOOST

MENTAL BOOST

ANTI-AGING: SKIN, HAIR & EYE HEALTH

DETOXIFY & MANAGE WEIGHT

ENERGY BOOST

83

ANTI-
INFLAMMATORY

IMMUNE BOOST

MENTAL BOOST

RELAXATION &
STRESS RELIEF

ANTI-AGING: SKIN,
HAIR & EYE HEALTH

DIGESTION

ENERGY BOOST

serves 1 to 2

# MANGO BANANA SLIDE

A super blend of good-for-you fruit helps keep your metabolism balanced and ready for jumping through hoops as needed.

½ CUP ICE CUBES
½ MANGO, PITTED, PEELED, CUT IN QUARTERS
½ MEDIUM RIPE BANANA, PEELED, CUT IN HALF
1 MANDARIN ORANGE, PEELED, SEGMENTED

**Place all of the of the ingredients in the Single Serve Cup and blend until smooth.**

per serving: cal 146; fat 0g; chol 0mg; sodium 5mg;
carb 38g; fiber 6g; protein 2g

 Bananas are loaded with potassium, which is good news for your heart.

serves 2

# WATERMELON KIWI SLUSH

Light, refreshing and a great way to beat the heat on a summer day. Use any kind of unsweetened fruit juice to change up this easy recipe.

½ CUP ICE CUBES
¾ CUP WATERMELON, CUT IN CHUNKS
1 KIWI, PEELED, CUT IN HALF
½ CUP WHITE GRAPE JUICE (OR ANY FRUIT JUICE)

**Place the ice, watermelon, kiwi and grape juice in the Single Serve Cup and blend until smooth.**

per serving: cal 161; fat 0g; chol 0mg; sodium 28mg; carb 42g; fiber 4g; protein 2g

 **tip** Watermelon is actually a vegetable related to pumpkin and squash, not a fruit!

ANTI-INFLAMMATORY

IMMUNE BOOST

MENTAL BOOST

RELAXATION & STRESS RELIEF

ANTI-AGING: SKIN, HAIR & EYE HEALTH

DETOXIFY & MANAGE WEIGHT

DIGESTION

ENERGY BOOST

serves 1 to 2

# THE FAT-BURNER

Berries are sometimes called "negative calorie" fruit because it takes more calories to digest and process them than they actually contain. Sort of like having your cake and eating it, too!

2 TO 3 ICE CUBES
½ CUP STRAWBERRIES, HULLED
¼ CUP RASPBERRIES
¼ CUP BLUEBERRIES
¼ CUP FILTERED WATER

**Place all of the of the ingredients in the Single Serve Cup and blend until smooth.**

per serving: cal 65; fat 0g; chol 0mg; sodium 2mg; carb 17g; fiber 3g; protein 2g

serves 4

# GRAPEFRUIT & STRAWBERRY CRUSH

Tangy grapefruit creates a kick in this smoothie, while gentle strawberry flavors calm it down. A winning combination!

1 CUP ICE CUBES
1 CUP FRESH STRAWBERRIES, HULLED
½ CUP GRAPEFRUIT, PEELED, SEGMENTED
12 OZ. STRAWBERRY YOGURT
4 TBSP. FILTERED WATER, PLUS MORE AS
    NEEDED

Place all of the ingredients in the pitcher and blend until smooth. If needed, add up to 2 tablespoons of water to reach your desired consistency.

per serving: cal 176; fat 0g; chol 0mg; sodium 106mg; carb 38g; fiber 2g; protein 8g

ANTI-INFLAMMATORY

IMMUNE BOOST

MENTAL BOOST

ANTI-AGING:SKIN, HAIR & EYE HEALTH

DETOXIFY & MANAGE WEIGHT

ENERGY BOOST

ANTI-INFLAMMATORY

IMMUNE BOOST

MENTAL BOOST

RELAXATION & STRESS RELIEF

ANTI-AGING: SKIN, HAIR & EYE HEALTH

DETOXIFY & MANAGE WEIGHT

DIGESTION

ENERGY BOOST

serves 3 to 4

# EMERALD GREEN ELIXIR

This could be the sweetest spinach you will ever drink!

1 CUP WHITE GRAPE JUICE
1 SMALL BANANA, PEELED
1 CUP BABY SPINACH LEAVES
2 KIWI, PEELED
4 TSP. RAW, UNFILTERED HONEY
10 TO 12 ICE CUBES

**Place all ingredients in the pitcher and blend until smooth. Serve right away.**

per serving: cal 220, fat 0g, chol 0mg, sodium 25mg,
carb 51g, fiber 4g, protein 2g

 Just 1 cup of spinach packs high
amounts of vitamins and minerals!

serves 2

# AVOCADO SHAKE

A creamy shake, irresistibly rich in flavor and filled with nutrients.

1 RIPE AVOCADO, PITTED AND PEELED
1 CUP LOWFAT MILK
2 TBSP. RAW, UNFILTERED HONEY
16 ICE CUBES

**Place all ingredients in the pitcher and blend until smooth.  Serve at once.**

per serving: cal 306, fat 16g, chol 6mg, sodium 483mg, carb 12g, fiber 7g, protein 16g

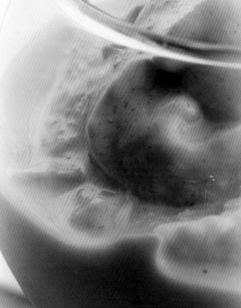

ANTI-INFLAMMATORY

MENTAL BOOST

RELAXATION & STRESS RELIEF

ANTI-AGING: SKIN, HAIR & EYE HEALTH

DIGESTION

ENERGY BOOST

ANTI-INFLAMMATORY

IMMUNE BOOST

MENTAL BOOST

RELAXATION & STRESS RELIEF

ANTI-AGING: SKIN, HAIR & EYE HEALTH

DETOXIFY & MANAGE WEIGHT

DIGESTION

ENERGY BOOST

serves 4

# VITAMIN C CUCUMBER BLAST

Get your fruit and veggie blast with this recipe.

2 GRAPEFUIT, PEELED AND QUARTERED
2 ORANGES, PEELED AND QUARTERED
½ CUCUMBER, PEELED
4 TO 6 ICE CUBES

Place all ingredients in the pitcher and blend until smooth.

per serving: cal 150, fat 0g, chol 0mg, sodium 1mg, carb 38g, fiber 6g, protein 3g

serves 3 to 4

# FRESH CITRUS SQUEEZE

Switch to any nonfat fruit-flavored yogurt  for a little change of "Citrus Squeeze".

½ CUP FRESH ORANGE JUICE
½ CUP FRESH RED GRAPEFRUIT,
   PEELED, SEGMENTED
1 CUP FRESH ORANGE, PEELED,
   SEGMENTED
1 CUP LOWFAT PLAIN YOGURT
2 TSP. POWDERED SUGAR
12 ICE CUBES

**Place all ingredients in the pitcher and blend until smooth. Serve right away.**

per serving: cal 201, fat 1g, chol 5mg, sodium 73mg, carb 45g, fiber 2g, protein 2g

ANTI-INFLAMMATORY

IMMUNE BOOST

MENTAL BOOST

RELAXATION & STRESS RELIEF

ANTI-AGING: SKIN, HAIR & EYE HEALTH

DETOXIFY & MANAGE WEIGHT

ENERGY BOOST

IMMUNE BOOST

MENTAL BOOST

ANTI-AGING: SKIN, HAIR & EYE HEALTH

DETOXIFY & MANAGE WEIGHT

ENERGY BOOST

serves 3 to 4

# WATERMELON & LIME SMOOTHIE

Summertime happiness – nothing better than refreshing watermelon on a hot afternoon.

1 CUP WHITE GRAPE JUICE
4 CUPS SEEDLESS WATERMELON CHUNKS, FROZEN
2 TSP. LIME ZEST (OPTIONAL)
4 TSP. RAW, UNFILTERED HONEY (OPTIONAL)

Place all ingredients in the pitcher and blend until smooth. Serve right away.

per serving: cal 141, fat 0g, chol 0mg, sodium 7mg, carb 37g, fiber 0g, protein 1g

ANTI-INFLAMMATORY

IMMUNE BOOST

RELAXATION & STRESS RELIEF

ANTI-AGING: SKIN, HAIR & EYE HEALTH

DETOXIFY & MANAGE WEIGHT

DIGESTION

serves 1

# PINEAPPLE PAPAYA SMOOTHIE

A tropical treat straight from the islands.

¼ CUP PAPAYA JUICE
½ CUP FRESH PINEAPPLE, CUT INTO CHUNKS
½ CUP FRESH PAPAYA
½ CUP LOWFAT VANILLA YOGURT
5 TO 6 ICE CUBES

**Place all of the of the ingredients in the Single Serve Cup and blend until smooth.**

per serving: cal 191, fat 1g, chol 5mg, sodium 79mg,
carb 41g, fiber 2g, protein 5g

ANTI-INFLAMMATORY

IMMUNE BOOST

RELAXATION & STRESS RELIEF

DETOXIFY & MANAGE WEIGHT

DIGESTION

ENERGY BOOST

serves 1

# GALA APPLE CELEBRATION

The collard greens put a southern twist on this nutritious drink!

½ CUP APPLE JUICE
½ RIPE GALA APPLE, CORED, ROUGHLY CUT
½ CUP COLLARD GREENS, RINSED, RIBS REMOVED
½ CUP NONFAT PLAIN YOGURT
PINCH GROUND CARDAMOM
5 TO 6 ICE CUBES

Place all of the of the ingredients in the Single Serve Cup and blend until smooth. Strain before serving, if desired.

per serving: cal 211, fat 0g, chol 0mg, sodium 97mg, carb 47g, fiber 4g, protein 7g

# EASY ENERGIZERS
*(boost your energy naturally)*

7

ANTI-INFLAMMATORY

IMMUNE BOOST

MENTAL BOOST

RELAXATION & STRESS RELIEF

ANTI-AGING: SKIN, HAIR & EYE HEALTH

DETOXIFY & MANAGE WEIGHT

DIGESTION

ENERGY BOOST

serves 1 to 2

# ENERGY BINGE

Depending on the season and what you have, use any combination of berries you like to equal the total amount used in this recipe. Toss in a handful of dried cranberries if you want to create a little surprise!

½ CUP ICE CUBES
¼ CUP BLACKBERRIES
¼ CUP BLUEBERRIES
¼ CUP RASPBERRIES
½ CUP RASPBERRY YOGURT
½ CUP CRANBERRY JUICE

**Place all of the of the ingredients in the Single Serve Cup and blend until smooth.**

per serving: cal 260; fat 2g; chol 5mg; sodium 134mg; carb 42g; fiber 6g; protein 8g

 **tip** Berries shouldn't be rinsed until just before eating them. To store, place them on a paper towel in a tightly-sealed container and refrigerate for up to 3 days.

serves 1 to 2

# ORANGEADE ALERT

Oranges have surprising properties that include strengthening your capillaries (the street map of your veins), helping prevent certain cancers, building immunity and aiding mental focus. The frozen vanilla yogurt in this recipe just adds to the goodness!

1 SMALL FROZEN ORANGE, PEELED, QUARTERED
    (OR USE SWEET MANDARIN ORANGES)
½ CUP FROZEN VANILLA YOGURT
½ CUP GRAPEFRUIT JUICE
1 TSP. HONEY

**Place all of the of the ingredients in the Single Serve Cup and blend until smooth.**

per serving: cal 226; fat 0g; chol 0mg; sodium 79mg; carb 58g; fiber 9g; protein 8g

 **tip** Look for a frozen yogurt brand that contains bacterial cultures!

ANTI-INFLAMMATORY

IMMUNE BOOST

MENTAL BOOST

RELAXATION & STRESS RELIEF

ANTI-AGING: SKIN, HAIR & EYE HEALTH

DETOXIFY & MANAGE WEIGHT

ENERGY BOOST

97

ANTI-INFLAMMATORY

IMMUNE BOOST

MENTAL BOOST

ANTI-AGING: SKIN, HAIR & EYE HEALTH

DETOXIFY & MANAGE WEIGHT

serves 1 to 2

# TOMATO SPIKE

This juice is a spike of zesty flavor!  Play with fire by adding more radishes or jalapeño pepper to suit your own taste.

2 TO 3 ICE CUBES
1 MEDIUM TOMATO, SEEDED, CUT IN HALF
½ CUP LOW-SODIUM TOMATO JUICE
2 RADISHES, STEMS REMOVED
¼ JALAPEÑO PEPPER, SEEDED

Place the ice, tomato, juice, radishes and pepper in the Single Serve Cup.
Blend until smooth.

per serving: cal 47; fat 0g; chol 0mg; sodium 76mg;
carb 10g; fiber 3g; protein 2g

serves 1 to 2

# SWEET BEET BLUSH

Our grandmothers knew all about beets, which is why a big bowl of beets were always on the table when we visited. Beets purify the blood and contain iron and vitamin B. We like them best when paired with oranges and a little dollop of honey, just like our grandmothers made them.

2 TO 3 ICE CUBES
½ SMALL FRESH BEET, PEELED, CUT IN CHUNKS
1 SMALL RIPE PLUM, PEELED, PITTED, QUARTERED
½ CUP ORANGE JUICE
1 TO 2 TSP. HONEY, OR TO TASTE

Place the ice, beet, plum, orange juice and honey in the Single Serve Cup. Blend until smooth. If desired, strain the juice before serving.

per serving: cal 131; fat 0g; chol 0mg; sodium 32mg; carb 32g; fiber 2g; protein 3g

IMMUNE BOOST

MENTAL BOOST

ANTI-AGING: SKIN, HAIR & EYE HEALTH

ENERGY BOOST

ANTI-INFLAMMATORY

IMMUNE BOOST

MENTAL BOOST

ANTI-AGING: SKIN, HAIR & EYE HEALTH

DETOXIFY & MANAGE WEIGHT

DIGESTION

ENERGY BOOST

serves 1 to 2

# RASPBERRY & GREEN TEA SURGE

Green tea is like a superhero in the antioxidant underworld. It helps your immune system and fights cancer cells as it refreshes and hydrates. Added to raspberries and mint, it becomes a divine elixir of the gods!

2 ICE CUBES
¾ CUP FRESH RASPBERRIES (OR USE
    STRAWBERRIES)
½ CUP SWEETENED GREEN TEA, COOLED
½ CUCUMBER, PEELED, CUT IN THIRDS
1 TBSP. MINT LEAVES

Place the ice, raspberries, sweetened tea, cucumber and mint in the Single Serve Cup. Blend until smooth.

per serving: cal 60; fat 1g; chol 0mg; sodium 3mg; carb 13g; fiber 7g; protein 2g

ANTI-INFLAMMATORY

IMMUNE BOOST

MENTAL BOOST

ANTI-AGING·SKIN, HAIR & EYE HEALTH

DETOXIFY & MANAGE WEIGHT

ENERGY BOOST

serves 1 to 2

# SPICY TOMATO JOLT

A tempting alternative to a Bloody Mary, this spicy juice awakens your senses in a big way.

2 TO 3 ICE CUBES
2 SMALL PLUM TOMATOES, CORED, CUT IN HALF
1 TSP. CREAMY HORSERADISH (OR USE
    CHINESE HOT MUSTARD), OR MORE TO TASTE
1 TSP. BALSAMIC VINEGAR
½ CUP WATER
½ SMALL CUCUMBER, PEELED, CUT IN CHUNKS
CRACKED BLACK PEPPER, OPTIONAL

Place all of the ingredients, except the black pepper, in the pitcher.  Blend until smooth.  Pour into glasses.  Add horseradish to taste and top with cracked black pepper.  Serve at once.

per serving: cal 37; fat 0g; chol 0mg; sodium 29mg; carb 8g; fiber 3g; protein 2g

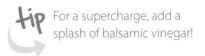

tip For a supercharge, add a splash of balsamic vinegar!

ANTI-INFLAMMATORY

IMMUNE BOOST

MENTAL BOOST

RELAXATION & STRESS RELIEF

ANTI-AGING: SKIN, HAIR & EYE HEALTH

DETOXIFY & MANAGE WEIGHT

ENERGY BOOST

serves 2 to 3

# VEGGIE FUSION

Tasty vegetables are even better when joined by an array of summer fruits.

¼ CUCUMBER, CUT INTO WEDGES
4 BABY CARROTS
2 STALK CELERY, CUT IN HALF
1 CUP SPINACH LEAVES, LIGHTLY PACKED
½ RIPE TOMATO
14 RED OR GREEN SEEDLESS GRAPES
1 TO 2 CUPS WATERMELON, CUT INTO CHUNKS
6 TO 8 ORANGE SLICES, PEELED
4 FRESH STRAWBERRIES (OR USE FROZEN)
4 TO 6 ICE CUBES

Place all the ingredients in the pitcher and blend until smooth.

per serving: cal 42, fat 0g, chol 0mg, sodium 32mg,
carb 19g, fiber 2g, protein 1g

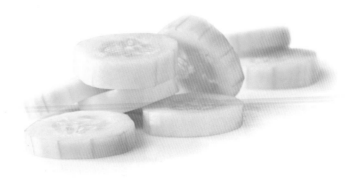

serves 4

# MOCHA FREEZE

A chocolate lovers dream…..pure chocolate satisfaction!

1 CUP STRONG COFFEE, COOLED
1 CUP LOWFAT CHOCOLATE FROZEN
    YOGURT
4 OZ. DARK CHOCOLATE
20 TO 24 ICE CUBES

Place all the ingredients in the pitcher and blend until smooth.  Serve right away.

per serving: cal 318, fat 13g, chol 17mg, sodium 85mg, carb 47g, fiber 5g, protein 7g

ANTI-INFLAMMATORY

MENTAL BOOST

RELAXATION & STRESS RELIEF

DETOXIFY & MANAGE WEIGHT

DIGESTION

ENERGY BOOST

serves 4

# COMPLETE WAKE-UP-CALL JUICE

Simply a burst of power in your day!

4 LARGE SWISS CHARD LEAVES
1 RIPE PEAR, CORED
12 MINT LEAVES
1 CUP WATER
8 TO 12 ICE CUBES

Place all the ingredients in the pitcher and blend until smooth.  Serve right away.

per serving: cal 57; fat 0g; chol 0mg; sodium 103mg; carb 15g; fiber 4g; protein 1g

serves 4

# COMPLETE SUNNY ENERGY JUICE

Cool citrus and apple cider vinegar blend into a bright pick-me up.

2 ORANGES, PEELED AND SECTIONED
2 TANGERINES, PEELED AND SECTIONED
4 TBSP. LEMON JUICE
4 TBSP. APPLE CIDER VINEGAR
2 TBSP. AGAVE (OPTIONAL)
12 TO 16 ICE CUBES

Place all ingredients in the pitcher and blend until smooth.  Serve right away.

per serving: cal 60; fat 0; chol 0mg; sodium 5mg;
carb 15g; fiber 3g; protein 4g

ANTI-INFLAMMATORY

IMMUNE BOOST

MENTAL BOOST

RELAXATION & STRESS RELIEF

ANTI-AGING: SKIN, HAIR & EYE HEALTH

DIGESTION

ENERGY BOOST

ANTI-INFLAMMATORY

IMMUNE BOOST

MENTAL BOOST

RELAXATION & STRESS RELIEF

ANTI-AGING: SKIN, HAIR & EYE HEALTH

DETOXIFY & MANAGE WEIGHT

DIGESTION

ENERGY BOOST

serves 4

# PINEAPPLE ENERGY SHAKE

A tropical energy delight! Use any seasonal fruit as substitutions.

1 CUP FRESH OR FROZEN PINEAPPLE,
   CUT IN CHUNKS
1 FRESH OR FROZEN MANGO, CUT IN CHUNKS
4 TBSP. FRESH LIME JUICE
1 CUP FRESH COCONUT MILK
6 TO 8 ICE CUBES

Place all of the ingredients in the pitcher and blend until smooth.  Serve right away.

per serving: cal 182; fat 12g; chol 0mg; sodium 10mg; carb 18g; fiber 1g; protein 4g

 **tip** Add 1 scoop of hemp protein for an extra lift!

serves 4

# BANANA COCONUT ENERGIZER

This delicious smoothie could actually be considered a dessert!

1 CUP FRESH OR FROZEN SHREDDED COCONUT
2 FROZEN BANANAS, PEELED, CUT IN HALF
2 OZ. DARK CHOCOLATE
4 PITTED DATES
2 CUPS LOWFAT MILK
4 TO 6 ICE CUBES

**Place all ingredients in the pitcher and blend until smooth. Serve at once.**

per serving: cal 65; fat 1g; chol 2mg; sodium 38mg; carb 12g; fiber 3g; protein 3g

 Add 1 scoop rice protein powder to get a super-sized burst of energy.

ANTI-INFLAMMATORY

IMMUNE BOOST

MENTAL BOOST

RELAXATION & STRESS RELIEF

DETOXIFY & MANAGE WEIGHT

DIGESTION

ENERGY BOOST

107

ANTI-INFLAMMATORY

IMMUNE BOOST

MENTAL BOOST

RELAXATION & STRESS RELIEF

ANTI-AGING: SKIN, HAIR & EYE HEALTH

DETOXIFY & MANAGE WEIGHT

DIGESTION

ENERGY BOOST

serves 1 to 2

# PAPAYA HABANERO POWER BLEND

Spicy and icy!

2 CUPS FRESH OR FROZEN PAPAYA, CUT IN CHUNKS
2 CUPS FRESH COCONUT MILK
2 TBSP. LIME JUICE
2 TBSP. AGAVE
1 TSP. FRESH HABANERO PEPPER, SEEDED
8 TO 10 ICE CUBES

Place all the ingredients in the pitcher and blend until smooth.  Serve right away.

per serving: cal 364; fat 29g; chol 20mg; sodium 35mg;
carb 35g; fiber 2g; protein 4g

# FROZEN ADULT INDULGENCES

*(responsibly, of course!)*

8

serves 2

# FRESH PAPAYA MOJITO FREEZE

Spiced rum gives this frozen cocktail a vanilla and caramelized sugar kick.

½ CUP ICE CUBES

2 OZ. SPICED RUM (SUCH AS CAPTAIN MORGAN®)

¼ RIPE PAPAYA, PEELED, SEEDED, CUT IN CHUNKS

2 OZ. CLUB SODA

1 TSP. LIME JUICE

1 TSP. SUGAR, OPTIONAL

4 MINT LEAVES

**Place all of the of the ingredients in the Single Serve Cup and blend until smooth.**

per serving: cal 142; fat 0g; chol 0mg; sodium 52mg; carb 3g; fiber 1g; protein 0g

serves 1

# COOL WATERMELON MARTINI

An excellent cocktail on July 5th, when you're sure to have leftover watermelon. And, what a great way to use those leftovers! If you like, place the prepared martini in the freezer until just icy around the edges of the glass.

½ CUP ICE CUBES
⅔ CUP WATERMELON, CUT IN CHUNKS
1 OZ. LEMON OR LIME VODKA (OR USE
    STANDARD VODKA)
1 OZ. TRIPLE SEC
1 TBSP. LIME JUICE
½ TSP. SUGAR, OPTIONAL
1 SLICE LIME WITH PEEL, FOR GARNISH

 Substitute 2/3 cup cucumber for the watermelon in this recipe for an unusual martini twist.

Place the watermelon in the Single Serve Cup and add the vodka, triple sec, juice and ice cubes. Add the sugar, if using. Blend until smooth. Pour into a martini glass and garnish with the lime slice.

per serving: cal 132; fat 0g; chol 0mg; sodium 1mg;
carb 12g; fiber 0g; protein 4g

ANTI-INFLAMMATORY

IMMUNE BOOST

MENTAL BOOST

RELAXATION & STRESS RELIEF

ANTI-AGING: SKIN, HAIR & EYE HEALTH

DETOXIFY & MANAGE WEIGHT

DIGESTION

ENERGY BOOST

ANTI-INFLAMMATORY

IMMUNE BOOST

MENTAL BOOST

RELAXATION & STRESS RELIEF

ANTI-AGING: SKIN, HAIR & EYE HEALTH

DETOXIFY & MANAGE WEIGHT

DIGESTION

ENERGY BOOST

serves 1 to 2

# RASPBERRY, STRAWBERRY & LEMON CRUSH

Refreshing, but not overly sweet, this cocktail is a superb thirst-quencher!

½ CUP ICE CUBES
2 OZ. GIN
2 FRESH BASIL LEAVES
2 TBSP. RASPBERRIES
3 TBSP. STRAWBERRIES, HULLED
1 TSP. LEMON JUICE
3 OZ. CLUB SODA

**Place all of the ingredients in the Single Serve Cup. Blend until smooth. Strain, if desired, before serving.**

per serving: cal 147; fat 0g; chol 0mg; sodium 76mg; carb 5g; fiber 2g; protein 0g

**tip** Basil is just about the easiest herb to plant and grow in a small kitchen garden. Keep it out of the cold and give it lots of sunlight to ensure plenty of fresh basil leaves for all your recipes.

serves 1

# PEACHY MARGARITA

Use only fully ripe peaches for this margarita recipe. For virgin margaritas, substitute orange juice for the tequila and peach schnapps.

½ CUP ICE CUBES

1 SMALL RIPE PEACH, PEELED, CUT IN CHUNKS

1 OZ. TEQUILA

½ OZ. PEACH SCHNAPPS (OR USE ½ OZ. TRIPLE SEC)

1 TSP. LIME JUICE

**Place all of the of the ingredients in the Single Serve Cup and blend until smooth.**

per serving: cal 147; fat 0g; chol 0mg; sodium 0mg; carb 12g; fiber 1g; protein 1g

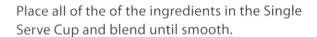

ANTI-INFLAMMATORY

IMMUNE BOOST

MENTAL BOOST

ANTI-AGING: SKIN, HAIR & EYE HEALTH

ANTI-INFLAMMATORY

IMMUNE BOOST

MENTAL BOOST

RELAXATION & STRESS RELIEF

ANTI-AGING: SKIN, HAIR & EYE HEALTH

ENERGY BOOST

serves 1

# BLUSHING ORANGE VODKA

Try substituting any type of flavored vodka with fresh fruit in this fun recipe.

3 TO 4 ICE CUBES
4 SECTIONS SWEET, RIPE ORANGE
2 OZ. ORANGE-FLAVORED VODKA
1 TSP. SUGAR
2 OZ. FRESH ORANGE JUICE
2 OZ. FRUITY RED WINE

Place the ice cubes, oranges, vodka, sugar and orange juice in the Single Serve Cup and blend until smooth.  Pour the mixture into a wine glass and float the red wine over the orange frost.  Do not stir; serve at once.

per serving: cal 263; fat 0g; chol 0mg; sodium 1mg; carb 11g; fiber 0g; protein 0g

serves 1

# ADULT-STRENGTH CHOCOLATE BANANA MILKSHAKE

A little boost of rum in this milkshake creates a memorable twist!

½ CUP CHOCOLATE FROZEN YOGURT
½ SMALL BANANA, PEELED
2 OZ. LIGHT RUM
2 TO 4 TBSP. LOWFAT MILK

Combine all ingredients in the Single Serve Cup.  Blend until smooth, adding milk as needed to make a pourable consistency.

per serving: cal 297; fat 2g; chol 5mg; sodium 95mg; carb 44g; fiber 4g; protein 6g

MENTAL BOOST

RELAXATION & STRESS RELIEF

DIGESTION

ENERGY BOOST

ANTI-INFLAMMATORY

IMMUNE BOOST

MENTAL BOOST

ANTI-AGING: SKIN, HAIR & EYE HEALTH

DETOXIFY & MANAGE WEIGHT

ENERGY BOOST

serves 2

# FROZEN RASPBERRY & PEACH COCKTAIL

A visually stunning cocktail, perfect for a bridal shower or any other celebration, large or small.

¼ CUP RASPBERRIES, FROZEN
½ CUP FROZEN PEACH CHUNKS
8 OZ. CHILLED PROSECCO
FRESH RASPBERRY FOR GARNISH

Place the frozen raspberries and peach chunks in the Single Serve Cup. Blend until smooth. Spoon the mixture into the bottom of 2 champagne flutes and top with chilled prosecco. Add a raspberry for garnish.

per serving: cal 103; fat 0g; chol 0mg; sodium 0mg; carb 7g; fiber 2g; protein 1g

serves 1

# FROZEN TEQUILA SLIDE

Keep several cubes of frozen limeade on hand for quick entertaining when surprise guests show up. Toss the cubes in the blender with a splash of tequila and you've got an instant party atmosphere.

½ CUP LIMEADE, FROZEN IN CUBES
1½ OZ. PREMIUM TEQUILA
2 TBSP. LEMON JUICE
1 TSP. COARSE SALT

Place the limeade cubes, tequila and lemon juice in the Single Serve Cup. Blend until smooth. Press the rim of short, wide glass in water, then in the coarse salt. Spoon the limeade mixture into the glass and serve.

per serving: cal 131; fat 0g; chol 0mg; sodium 468mg; carb 9g; fiber 0g; protein 0g

ANTI-INFLAMMATORY

IMMUNE BOOST

MENTAL BOOST

RELAXATION & STRESS RELIEF

ANTI-AGING: SKIN, HAIR & EYE HEALTH

DETOXIFY & MANAGE WEIGHT

DIGESTION

ENERGY BOOST

serves 4

# BLUEBERRY CAIPIROSKA

This drink will make you want to dance the night away....Brazilian style.

1 CUP FRESH BLUEBERRIES, WASHED
8 OZ. VODKA
16 ICE CUBES
8 LARGE MINT LEAVES FOR GARNISH

**Place all ingredients in the pitcher and blend until smooth.**

per serving: cal 161; fat 0g; chol 0mg; sodium 1mg; carb 4g; fiber 1g; protein 0g

serves 4

# HONEYDEW MELON GIMLET

A quintessential summer drink.

1 CUP HONEYDEW MELON, IN CHUNKS
2 TSP. FRESH LIME JUICE
8 OZ. DRY GIN
4 SLICES FRESH LIME (OPTIONAL)
ICE CUBES

Place the melon, juice and gin in the pitcher and blend until smooth. Strain before serving, if desired. Pour over ice cubes and garnish with lime slices.

per serving: cal 146, fat 0g, chol 0mg, sodium 9mg, carb 6g, fiber 1g, protein 1g

ANTI-AGING: SKIN, HAIR & EYE HEALTH

DETOXIFY & MANAGE WEIGHT

DIGESTION

ANTI-INFLAMMATORY

IMMUNE BOOST

RELAXATION & STRESS RELIEF

ANTI-AGING: SKIN, HAIR & EYE HEALTH

DETOXIFY & MANAGE WEIGHT

DIGESTION

ENERGY BOOST

serves 4

# HARD APPLE POMEGRANATE CIDER

A perfect fall, winter or holiday drink to sip by the fireplace.

1 RIPE RED DELICIOUS APPLE, CORED,
    ROUGHLY CUT
8 OZ. APPLE BRANDY
½ CUP POMEGRANATE JUICE
1 CUP APPLE CIDER
2 CINNAMON STICKS

Place the apple in the pitcher and blend until smooth. Add the brandy, juice and cider and blend again until smooth. Strain, if desired.

Pour the cider into a large saucepan and add the cinnamon sticks. Heat on medium-low until simmering, stirring occasionally. Remove the cinnamon sticks and ladle into four heatproof mugs. Serve right away.

per serving: cal 184, fat 0g, chol 0mg, sodium 30mg, carb 32g, fiber 0g, protein 0g

serves 4

# TROPICAL SUNSET SPARKLER

You don't need a special occasion to enjoy this drink. Cheers!

20 ICE CUBES
½ CUP ORANGE JUICE
½ CUP PINEAPPLE JUICE
12 OZ. PROSECCO OR CHAMPAGNE
4 TBSP. GRENADINE
4 FRESH SWEET CHERRIES

Place the ice cubes in the pitcher and blend until completely smooth. Divide the powdered ice evenly among four cocktail glasses.

Place the orange juice, pineapple juice, and Prosecco in the pitcher and blend until smooth. Pour equally over the ice. Do not stir or mix. Drizzle 1 tablespoon of grenadine over the top of each cocktail and top with a cherry.

per serving: cal 262, fat 0g, chol 0mg, sodium 10mg, carb 45g, fiber 0g, protein 2g

ANTI-INFLAMMATORY

IMMUNE BOOST

MENTAL BOOST

RELAXATION & STRESS RELIEF

ANTI-AGING: SKIN, HAIR & EYE HEALTH

ENERGY BOOST

ANTI-INFLAMMATORY

IMMUNE BOOST

MENTAL BOOST

ANTI-AGING: SKIN, HAIR & EYE HEALTH

DETOXIFY & MANAGE WEIGHT

ENERGY BOOST

serves 4

# HARD RASPBERRY & MINT LEMONADE

This isn't your grandma's lemonade.

8 OZ. VODKA

8 OZ. CLUB SODA

½ CUP LEMONADE

½ CUP FRESH RASPBERRIES, RINSED

2 TBSP. POWDERED SUGAR

4 MINT LEAVES

ICE CUBES

Place all the ingredients, except the ice cubes, in the pitcher and blend. Fill 4 cocktail glasses with ice cubes and pour the lemonade over each. Serve right away.

per serving: cal 190, fat 0g, chol 0mg, sodium 10mg, carb 12g, fiber 0g, protein 0g

serves 4

# REFRESHING CUCUMBER & MINT CHAMPAGNE COCKTAILS

Beautiful and good for you!

1 SMALL CUCUMBER, PEELED, QUARTERED
6 LARGE MINT LEAVES
2 TBSP. RAW, UNFILTERED HONEY
2 OZ. MIDORI
12 OZ. DRY CHAMPAGNE, CHILLED

Place the cucumber, mint leaves and honey in the pitcher and blend until smooth. Add the Midori and champagne and blend again. Strain and pour into champagne glasses. Serve right away.

per serving: cal 137, fat 0g, chol 0mg, sodium 1mg, carb 8g, fiber 1g, protein 1g

ANTI-INFLAMMATORY

IMMUNE BOOST

ANTI-AGING, SKIN, HAIR & EYE HEALTH

DIGESTION

ENERGY BOOST

ANTI-INFLAMMATORY

IMMUNE BOOST

MENTAL BOOST

RELAXATION & STRESS RELIEF

ANTI-AGING: SKIN, HAIR & EYE HEALTH

DETOXIFY & MANAGE WEIGHT

DIGESTION

ENERGY BOOST

serves 6

# RUM & HONEYDEW AGUA FRESCA

Agua Fresca is readily available in Mexico and is now starting to make an appearance in juice bars north of the border. Easy to make, it is delightfully refreshing!

4 CUPS HONEYDEW MELON, CUT IN CHUNKS
½ CUP WATER
¼ CUP HONEY
2 TBSP. LIME JUICE
18 MINT LEAVES, MUDDLED IN GLASSES
8 OZ. RUM
3 CUPS ICE CUBES
12 MELON BALLS THREADED ON 6 WOODEN
    SKEWERS

Place the honeydew, water, honey and lime juice in the pitcher and blend until very smooth. Muddle a few mint leaves in bottom of each of 6 glasses and fill each with ice cubes. Add a shot of rum to each glass and pour drink over ice, straining if desired. Garnish with melon skewers.

per serving: cal 168; fat 0g; chol 0mg; sodium 32mg; carb 27g; fiber 1g; protein 1g

serves 3 to 4

# BERRYLICIOUS COLADA

Rich with antioxodiants and delightful berry flavor!

1 CUP FROZEN BLUEBERRIES
½ CUP FRESH BLACKBERRIES
1 CUP BLACKBERRY SORBET
¾ CUP LIGHT CREAM
6 OZ. LIGHT RUM
2 TSP. LEMON JUICE
1 CUP ICE CUBES (9 TO 10 CUBES)
12 TO 16 BLACKBERRIES, FROSTED, SKEWERED AND
    FROZEN

Place all ingredients, except blackberry garnish, in the pitcher and blend until smooth. Pour into stemmed cocktail glasses and garnish with blackberry skewers.

per serving: cal 254; fat 6g; chol 17mg; sodium 55mg;
carb 24g; fiber 4g; protein 3g

ANTI-INFLAMMATORY

IMMUNE BOOST

MENTAL BOOST

RELAXATION & STRESS RELIEF

ANTI-AGING: SKIN, HAIR & EYE HEALTH

DETOXIFY & MANAGE WEIGHT

DIGESTION

ENERGY BOOST

ANTI-
INFLAMMATORY

IMMUNE BOOST

MENTAL BOOST

RELAXATION &
STRESS RELIEF

ANTI-AGING: SKIN,
HAIR & EYE HEALTH

serves 3 to 4

# RIPE PLUM PARADISE

The name says it all; this drink is paradise!

1 FRESH, RIPE PLUM, PITTED
4 OZ. PLUM BRANDY
1 OZ. ORANGE LIQUEUR
8 OZ. DARK RUM
 ICE CUBES

Place the plum, brandy, liqueur and rum in the pitcher and blend until smooth.
Pour over the ice cubes before serving.

per serving: cal 231; fat 0g; chol 0mg; sodium 1mg;
carb 7g; fiber 0g; protein 4g

# DECADENTLY DELICIOUS

*(cold fusion's finest)*

9

serves 1 to 2

# PEANUT BUTTER CRUNCH

Well-suited for those teenagers who can't seem to get out of bed in the morning. This smoothie is loaded with protein and natural goodness so it's a super start to any day of the week.

½ CUP ICE CUBES
½ CUP LOWFAT MILK (OR USE WHOLE OR
    NONFAT MILK)
3 TBSP. CRUNCHY PEANUT BUTTER (OR ADD 1
    TBSP. PEANUTS TO CREAMY PEANUT BUTTER)
½ CUP SOFT TOFU (OR USE SILKEN TOFU)
2 TSP. HONEY
1 TO 2 TBSP. ALL-NATURAL CRUNCHY CEREAL,
    OPTIONAL (USE CEREAL SUCH AS KASHI™)

Place all of the ingredients, except the honey and cereal, in the Single Serve Cup. Blend until smooth. Spoon the smoothie into glasses and garnish with a swirl of honey and a spoonful of cereal, if using. Serve right away.

per serving: cal 205; fat 2g; chol 7mg; sodium 123mg; carb 40g; fiber 0g; protein 8g

MENTAL BOOST

DETOXIFY & MANAGE WEIGHT

DIGESTION

ENERGY BOOST

serves 2

# SPICED APPLE PIE

Sometimes we want an especially satisfying, yet light juice blend. This is a provocative combination of pie spices and apples that reminds us of the holidays.

½ RIPE APPLE, CORED, CUT IN CHUNKS
¾ CUP WATER
1 SMALL BOSC PEAR, CORED, PEELED,
    CUT IN CHUNKS
DASH GROUND CINNAMON
DASH GROUND CLOVES
2 CINNAMON STICKS, OPTIONAL

Place the apple, water, pear, cinnamon and cloves in the Single Serve Cup. Blend until smooth. Serve or heat gently just until warm before serving. Garnish with whole cinnamon sticks, if desired.

per serving: cal 143; fat 0g; chol 0mg; sodium 4mg;
carb 39g; fiber 7g; protein 1g

ANTI-INFLAMMATORY

IMMUNE BOOST

RELAXATION & STRESS RELIEF

DETOXIFY & MANAGE WEIGHT

DIGESTION

ENERGY BOOST

IMMUNE BOOST

serves 1 to 2

# PEACHES N' CREAM SMOOTHIE

Rich and delicious, this smoothie works as a breakfast indulgence or simple dessert.

½ RIPE PEACH, PEELED, PITTED, CUT IN CHUNKS
½ CUP VANILLA FROZEN YOGURT
½ CUP LIGHT CREAM (OR USE MILK)
2 TBSP. HONEY
PINCH GROUND CINNAMON

**Place all of the ingredients in the Single Serve Cup and blend until smooth.**

per serving: cal 383; fat 14g; chol 46mg; sodium 120mg; carb 65g; fiber 5g; protein 11g

ANTI-AGING: SKIN, HAIR & EYE HEALTH

serves 1 to 2

# MAPLE PRALINE SMOOTHIE

The subtle essence of maple, along with the pecans, adds a sweet twist on a simple smoothie.

2 TBSP. PECANS, SHELLED
½ SMALL BANANA, PEELED
¾ CUP VANILLA FROZEN YOGURT
1 TSP. MAPLE SYRUP

**Place all of the ingredients in the Single Serve Cup and blend until smooth.**

per serving: cal 291; fat 9g; chol 0mg; sodium 151mg; carb 51g; fiber 8g; protein 8g

 Eating about 1½ ounces of pecans daily actually helps lower your LDL cholesterol counts.

MENTAL BOOST

RELAXATION & STRESS RELIEF

DIGESTION

ENERGY BOOST

IMMUNE BOOST

MENTAL BOOST

ANTI-AGING: SKIN, HAIR & EYE HEALTH

DIGESTION

ENERGY BOOST

serves 4

# MANGO PEACH FROZEN YOGURT

Cold, tart and very creamy.

½ CUP FROZEN MANGO CHUNKS
½ CUP FROZEN PEACHES
2 CUPS LOWFAT VANILLA YOGURT

Place the mango, peaches and yogurt in the pitcher. Blend until smooth. Serve right away.

per serving: cal 102; fat 2g; chol 2mg; sodium 85mg; carb 5g; fiber 1g; protein 12g

makes about 1 quart

# STRAWBERRY BASIL ICE CREAM

Perfect for a midnight raid to the freezer.

2 CUPS STRAWBERRIES, STEMMED AND HULLED
1 CUP SUGAR
15 FRESH BASIL LEAVES
2 CUPS WHOLE MILK
2 CUPS LIGHT CREAM
2 TSP. VANILLA EXTRACT

Place the strawberries, sugar and basil in the pitcher. Blend until the strawberry mixture is smooth. Spoon into a large bowl, add the remaining ingredients and stir to combine.

Pour the ice cream mixture into the freezer bowl or tub of your ice cream maker and proceed as directed.

per serving: cal 225; fat 9g; chol 29mg; sodium 50mg; carb 34g; fiber 1g; protein 4g

ANTI-INFLAMMATORY

IMMUNE BOOST

MENTAL BOOST

ANTI-AGING: SKIN, HAIR & EYE HEALTH

DETOXIFY & MANAGE WEIGHT

ENERGY BOOST

ANTI-INFLAMMATORY

IMMUNE BOOST

MENTAL BOOST

RELAXATION & STRESS RELIEF

ANTI-AGING: SKIN, HAIR & EYE HEALTH

DIGESTION

ENERGY BOOST

serves 6

# FRUIT N' CREAM ICE CREAM

Homemade ice cream the easy way.

2 CUPS FROZEN FRUIT (MIXED BERRIES,
    STRAWBERRIES, PEACHES ETC.)
½ CUP HEAVY CREAM (OR USE MILK OR
    LOWFAT MILK)
2 TO 4 TBSP. SUGAR
1 TSP. VANILLA EXTRACT

## Place all ingredients in the pitcher. Blend until smooth.

per serving: cal 161; fat 11g; chol 41mg; sodium 12mg;
carb 15g; fiber 1g; protein 0g

**tip** Try frozen bananas, pitted cherries or even avocados for a special dessert!

serves 4

# FRESH MANGO FOOL

A small serving of sweet mango and cream creates a memorable dessert.

2 MANGOS, PEELED AND SEEDED
½ CUP SUGAR SYRUP
1 CUP WHIPPED CREAM

Place the mangos and sugar syrup in the pitcher and blend until smooth. Spoon the mango mixture into a medium bowl and fold in the whipped cream. Serve right away in stemmed glasses.

per serving: cal 182; fat 11g; chol 21mg; sodium 14mg; carb 29g; fiber 2g; protein 2g

MENTAL BOOST

ANTI-AGING: SKIN, HAIR & EYE HEALTH

DETOXIFY & MANAGE WEIGHT

ENERGY BOOST

serves 4

# CANTALOUPE MINT GRANITA

Vitamin A, Vitamin C - cantaloupe has it all.

1 RIPE CANTALOUPE, SEEDED, RIND REMOVED,
    AND CUT INTO CHUNKS
1 TBSP. FRESH LEMON JUICE
2 TBSP. WATER
2 TBSP. RAW, UNFILTERED HONEY
1 TBSP. FRESH MINT LEAVES

Place all of the ingredients in the pitcher and blend until completely smooth. Pour into a non-reactive dish or ice cube trays and freeze for 3 to 4 hours, until completely solid.

Just before serving, place the frozen cubes in the pitcher and blend again until smooth. Serve immediately.

per serving: cal 79; fat 0g; chol 0mg; sodium 85mg; carb 22g; fiber 1g; protein 2g

makes about 1 quart

# PINEAPPLE GINGER COCONUT SORBET

A great dessert for an elegant meal.

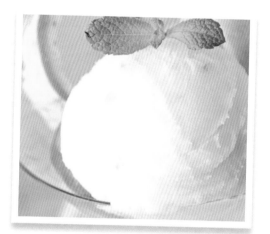

1 SMALL RIPE PINEAPPLE, PEELED, CORED,
    ROUGHLY CUT
1 TBSP. FRESH LIME JUICE
½ CUP LIGHT COCONUT MILK
½ CUP SUPERFINE SUGAR
1 TSP. FRESH GINGER, CHOPPED

Place the pineapple in the pitcher and blend until smooth. Pour into a medium bowl. Place all of the remaining ingredients in the pitcher. Blend until completely smooth and add to the pineapple. Stir lightly to mix.

Pour the sorbet mixture into the freezer bowl or tub of your ice cream maker and proceed as directed.

per serving: cal 114; fat 1g; chol 0mg; sodium 4mg;
carb 28g; fiber 2g; protein 1g

ANTI-INFLAMMATORY

IMMUNE BOOST

RELAXATION & STRESS RELIEF

ANTI-AGING: SKIN, HAIR & EYE HEALTH

DETOXIFY & MANAGE WEIGHT

DIGESTION

ENERGY BOOST

ANTI-INFLAMMATORY

IMMUNE BOOST

MENTAL BOOST

RELAXATION & STRESS RELIEF

ANTI-AGING: SKIN, HAIR & EYE HEALTH

DETOXIFY & MANAGE WEIGHT

DIGESTION

ENERGY BOOST

makes about 1 quart

# TART BLUEBERRY SORBET

Blueberries....a boost of antioxidants........enjoy!

5 CUPS FROZEN BLUEBERRIES
½ CUP RAW, UNFILTERED HONEY
1 TSP. LEMON ZEST
1 TBSP. LEMON JUICE

Working in batches if needed, blend the blueberries in the pitcher until smooth. Place the blueberries in a large mixing bowl and add the honey, zest and juice. Mix well and place in your ice cream maker. Proceed as directed.

per serving: cal 86; fat 0g; chol 0mg; sodium 1mg; carb 28g; fiber 1g; protein 0g

serves 4

# GREEN TEA GRANITA

The miracle of Green Tea......better to be deprived of food for three days, than tea for one....

3 CUPS WATER
3 GREEN TEA BAGS
¼ CUP RAW, UNFILTERED HONEY
1 TBSP. FRESH LEMON JUICE
FRESH MINT FOR GARNISH

Bring the water to a boil in a saucepan. Add the green tea and honey. Let steep for 15 minutes. Remove tea bags. Let cool and add the lemon juice. Mix to combine. Pour into ice cube trays. Let freeze for at least 3 hours, or until solid.

Place the frozen tea ice cubes in the pitcher and blend for 30 seconds. Garnish with mint leaves and serve immediately.

per serving: Cal 129; FaT 0g; CHOL 0Mg; sodium 1MG; Carb 35g; fiber 0g; Protein 0g

ANTI-INFLAMMATORY

IMMUNE BOOST

ANTI-AGING: SKIN, HAIR & EYE HEALTH

DETOXIFY & MANAGE WEIGHT

DIGESTION

serves 4 to 6

# SUMMER PEACHY ICE CREAM

When summer peaches are ripe and readily available at the farmers market, this is a perfect peachy way to enjoy them.

3 CUPS FROZEN PEACHES, PITTED, CUT IN HALF
1 CUP LIGHT CREAM
3 TBSP. MAPLE SYRUP
¼ TSP. CINNAMON

Place all ingredients in the pitcher and blend until very smooth. Serve immediately or store in an airtight container in the freezer.

per serving: cal 113; fat 5g; chol 15mg; sodium 18mg; carb 17g; fiber 1g; protein 2g

serves 4

# BERRY MINT SORBET

A sweet refresher to an elegant meal.

1 CUP SUGAR
1 CUP WATER
2 SPRIGS MINT
4 CUPS MIXED FROZEN BERRIES
2 TBSP. LEMON JUICE

In a small saucepan over medium heat, bring sugar, water and mint to a boil, stirring to dissolve sugar. Set aside and, when cool, remove mint sprigs.

Place berries, cooled liquid and lemon juice in the pitcher and blend until very smooth. Serve immediately or store in an airtight container in the freezer.

per serving: cal 264; fat 0g; chol 0mg; sodium 0mg;
carb 68g; fiber 5g; protein 0g

ANTI-INFLAMMATORY

IMMUNE BOOST

MENTAL BOOST

RELAXATION & STRESS RELIEF

ANTI-AGING: SKIN, HAIR & EYE HEALTH

DETOXIFY & MANAGE WEIGHT

DIGESTION

ENERGY BOOST

# INDEX